Relaxation

A Complete Guide for Body Relaxing Including Aromatherapy and Massage Therapy

AROMATHERAPY

A Comprehensive Guide to Get Started with Essential Oils

Jessica Thompson

DISCLAIMER

This information is for reference purposes only.

Statements are not intended as a substitute for professional healthcare nor meant to diagnose, treat, cure or prevent medical conditions or disease.

Every illness or injury requires supervision by a medical doctor or an alternative medicine practitioner.

CONTENTS

1 HISTORY AND TRADITION 7

2 AROMATHERAPY & ESSENTIAL OILS DECODED 11

3 ESSENTIAL OILS BUYING GUIDE 19

4 WAYS TO USE ESSENTIAL OILS 23

5 GENERAL SAFETY PRECAUTIONS 27

6 TWELVE ESSENTIAL OIL RELAXANTS 29

7 THE BASIC ESSENTIAL OILS 40

© Copyright 2018 by Jessica Thompson

All rights reserved.

The following eBook is reproduced below with the goal of providing information that is as accurate and reliable as possible. Regardless, purchasing this eBook can be seen as consent to the fact that both the publisher and the author of this book are in no way experts on the topics discussed within and that any recommendations or suggestions that are made herein are for entertainment purposes only. Professionals should be consulted as needed prior to undertaking any of the action endorsed herein.

This declaration is deemed fair and valid by both the American Bar Association and the Committee of Publishers Association and is legally binding throughout the United States.

Furthermore, the transmission, duplication or reproduction of any of the following work including specific information will be considered an illegal act irrespective of if it is done electronically or in print. This extends to creating a secondary or tertiary copy of the work or a recorded copy and is only allowed with an expressed written consent from the Publisher. All additional rights reserved.

The information in the following pages is broadly considered to be truthful and accurate account of facts, and as such any inattention, use or misuse of the information in question by the reader will render any resulting actions solely under their purview. There are no scenarios in which the publisher or the original author of this work can be in any fashion deemed liable for any hardship or damages that may befall them after undertaking information described herein.

Additionally, the information in the following pages is intended only for informational purposes and should thus be thought of as universal. As befitting its nature, it is presented without assurance regarding its prolonged validity or interim quality. Trademarks that are mentioned are done without written consent and can in no way be considered an endorsement from the trademark holder.

1
HISTORY AND TRADITION

Plants are not only incredible sources of nutrients and foods for man, present in them are also many of nature's wondrous components that have extremely been helpful in solving man's most challenging health conditions. Plants contain numerous phytonutrients which and among other things, include a plethora of extracts that have a phenomenal aromatic essence, for example essential oils. Sometimes dubbed the "soul" of plants, essential oils have long been a mainstay in many culinary and therapeutic preparations. In contrast to its name, essential oils don't typically present as oils from the outside; they appear more watery, and so less viscous than would be expected of oils. That said, essential oils are extremely volatile and highly concentrated, and so are usually laden with a wide range of organic components.

Vitamins, hormone and certain chemicals fall into the group of essential oils needed by plants to successfully carry out life functions. For example, flowers have essences that help them attract plants, and this is vitally important for their pollination. In shrub trees, resin is the essential oil that helps to heal wounds faster while providing enough resistance when extremes of weather set in. Essential oils help to keep the plant moist by preventing excessive water evaporation. But that's not all, they can also help plants to ward off predatory attacks by serving as a deterrent to external aggressors while communicating the danger to nearby plants and trees.

Due to their wide range of components and aesthetic presence, essential oils have long been used by man in the preparation of air fresheners, as food enrichment and also medically, to heal the body of many conditions.

The medical use of essential oils dates back to thousands of years ago where they were included in the practice of aromatherapy. Shen Nung, a Legendary Chinese ruler, is credited with the initial efforts that brought the medicinal properties of plants to fore. He wrote 'Pen Tsao' (c. 2700-3000 BC) - the first written herbal text that contained over two hundred botanicals. His initial findings sparked curiosity among archaeologists and scientists alike, making civilizations in China, the Middle East and India explore the therapeutic benefits of essential oils during these early periods. For example, a traditional Hindu form of healing called Ayurveda is synonymous with the use of local herbs in the treatment of many conditions.

In Ancient Egypt, waters, incense, resins and ointments were extensively used in religious ceremonies. It is also believed that Queen Cleopatra also had massive collections of flowers in her garden, and used the essences obtained therefrom for perfuming herself and surroundings. Pharaohs were strongly linked with the use of Terra cotta urns. And in Rome, soldiers found the magical benefits of honey and used it alongside myrrh to heal wounds. Roman emperors fancied perfumed baths as it gave the much-needed relaxation and soothing feeling. Both Old and New Testaments of the Bible also contain recipes that had aromatic compounds in their preparation.

In Europe, widespread exploration and use of essential oils were facilitated in the 16th century when glass distillation methods were discovered. More robust trade routes and the invention of the microscope meant bioactive compounds could also be better studied. Hence, extraction of plant essential oils became popular in plants like Italian chamomile, French rosemary and English lavender. Queen Elizabeth I is known to have used an overwhelming supply of English lavender oil during the course of her reign, and the tradition was continued throughout the 64-year rule of Queen Victoria.

The early 20th century brought aromatherapy to life in modern history as French chemist Rene-Maurice Gattesfosse who, inadvertently, set his arm ablaze in the laboratory was relieved after dipping his hands in the closest vat of cold liquid, coincidentally lavender oil. While previous injuries from chemical burns brought extended and deep pains, blisters, inflammation induced redness and scarring, Gattesfosse's burn surprisingly didn't present similar problems, with only slight pains and no scarring. It was obvious this had something to do with the lavender oil, and so reckoned Gattefosse too. This intriguing observation led him to coin 'aromatherapy,' a word he used to describe the exceptional healing he had received.

But he wasn't going to let the knowledge of lavender oil go down the drain, and so he dedicated many more years in the research of the attendant health benefits of essentials which culminated in his well-known book "Aromatherapy" that was published in 1937. In it, Gattefosse stated his findings on essential oils, and consequently further brought the medical use of these agents to limelight. With the book becoming a staple in the collections of essential oil enthusiasts, the work was translated into English in 1993. Unsurprisingly, the second edition is still available in print after 70 years.

Gattefosse efforts meant other scientists like Jean Valnet, a French physician, delved deeper into essential oils. Valnet chose to use essential oils in helping heal wounds during World War II. Soldiers that would have otherwise been amputated were able to successfully manage their injuries by getting treated with essential oils. Jean's book 'The Practice of Aromatherapy' further advanced the cause of essential oils as it made the oils become widely accepted, ensuring they were adopted for medical and psychiatric use in France in the 1960s. Marguerite Maury published more discoveries on essential oils in 1962, and so these oils gradually became mainstream ingredients in the cosmetic industry. Robert Tisserand's 'The Art of Aromatherapy' provided the springboard for the popularity of aromatherapy and massage, propelling them to become a common practice throughout the United Kingdom and the United States.

The popularity of aromatherapy, as it gradually spread to other parts of the world, coupled with the dynamic rise of natural medicines in the 1980s ensured its reliability as a health regimen which has since gone on to become a veritable way of treating many health conditions. So much so that in 2008, it accounted for about 95% of the world's essential oils market, translating to close to US$ 4.6-billion. The aromatherapy industry has consistently grown ever since at the rate of 7.5% annually over the last decade, and the trend may not go down south anytime soon with everyone getting on board to have a feel of the unrivaled natural healing experience.

2
AROMATHERAPY & ESSENTIAL OILS DECODED

First off, aromatherapy is not supposed to be a one-size-fits-all substitute for all conditions where traditional medical treatment is intended. While its activity has been well documented, aromatherapy is only an extension of a long-running practice involving the use of plants to treat medical conditions. For example, the aspirin we use today was a product of experiments conducted at the Bayer & Co dye factory using a byproduct obtained from the spirea plant.

Chemist Felix Hoffman is credited with synthesizing the first known acetylsalicylic acid which had earlier been known to be helpful in the treatment of rheumatism. Cold colds are a common bane, but we've also been able to successfully remedy the condition using Vicks Vaporub whose active ingredients are synthetic forms of many products including laurel tree i.e camphor, mint (menthol), and eucalyptus as well as nutmeg, cedar leaf and pine oils. Coca-Cola was initially marketed as a product that served as a 'nerve tonic,' with ingredients including essential oils of spices and citrus fruits.

Aromatherapy is interestingly an amazing science, but it is also an art, making it an exhilarating but equally daunting task when studying the nitty-gritty of its wide scope. On the whole, essential oils are a group of aromatic molecules gotten from plant part and materials like leaves, petals, needles, twigs, seeds, resin, wood and rind. Here are basic concepts and terms to easily understand the nuances of the pharmacological and botanical data in the study of Aromatherapy.

ABSOLUTE OILS

Absolute oils are the semi-liquid or alcohol soluble oils gotten from plants with a solvent extraction process that produces very low yield.

For example, a thousand pounds of flowers yield only about one teaspoon of jasmine absolute. A teaspoon of "rose absolute" can be gotten from around five thousand pounds of petals. With distillation, however, an equal amount of ottor (attar), a rose essential oil requires a staggering ten thousand pounds of petals. Hence, rose otto costs expectedly twice as much the price of rose absolute regarded to be among the most expensive essential oils.

BLENDED OILS

Blended oils are essentially a recipe or formula that is derived from synergizing or combining a host of essential oils. The selection of blended oils is literally unlimited with more than enough options abound. Expert aromatherapists also have their own preferred combinations or recipes usually advised by their extensive knowledge and experience.

While going with blends comes across as a great way to experiment with pre- combined formulas, it may however be time-consuming, so learning the essential oils and putting ideas into practice is a trusty way of getting a reliable mix for any medical condition or purpose. Thus, blended remedies may appear as having the same ingredient composition, however, they will almost always not be combined in the same proportion.

CARRIER OIL

Essentials oils are characteristically thin and watery, but even if they are unusually thick, there's little to no chance of having them dissolve in water. Essential oils are only exceedingly soluble in alcohol or fatty oils. Carrier oils are used to dilute essential oils, and are sometimes referred to as base oil. They include products from a number of sources like nuts, seeds, trees or vegetables. Popular carrier oils are those of coconut, almond, sunflower and jojoba.

Blends of essential oils are usually composed of a carrier oil combined with minute quantities of essentials since essential oils on their own are noticeably too harsh to be used when not diluted, or too costly to be used without a carrier oil. However, a few of these oils can be used as carrier oils, examples of which include tea tree or lavender. Apart from making for more seamless application, carrier oils are great for keeping the moisture of essential oils on the skin for extended periods. Besides, diluted essential oils are long lasting as only small quantities are needed during the massage process.

EXTRACTION

The term "Extraction" refers to the process of obtaining oil molecules stored in plants. Understanding the extraction process is key to knowing the inherent properties of an oil. It also tells more about its benefits as well as ways to purchase and use. Extraction of oil molecules from plants can be carried out in many ways. These include steam or water distillation, expression, or by solvent extraction.

- **Steam or Water Distillation**
  Steam distillation using pressure remains one of the most efficient processes of extraction. Here, the plant is heated, and as formed vapor cools, essential oil is what is obtained. On the other hand, water distillation involves covering the plant material in water and subsequently heating up the plant. Distillation by water takes a longer time to go to completion, and therefore comes with the risk of losing essential oil components that are not overly resistant to heat, making steam distillation the more preferred extraction method.

- **Solvent extraction**
  This process of extraction is a great alternative when sensitive parts like jasmine and rose petals are the source of essential oil. Solvent extraction ends a method known as enfleurage where glass placed petals are covered with an odorless fat or oil. On the alternative, flowers can be stirred into heated oil. A "pomade" or "concrete" is formed when enough flowers have saturated the oil or fat. The pomade formed afterward is soaked in alcohol to absorb the fragrance produced by the fat, and the two are then separated. As the alcohol evaporates, the particulate plant matter

is left behind. This is what is referred to as the flower's "absolute" essence. The fat is used in the manufacturing of soap. If benzene, hexane, or other synthetic petrochemical is used as a solvent, the "absolute" essence gotten from the process comes with fewer benefits than alcohol - a sugar derived organic substance.

- **Expression**
  This is used for oil extraction from the rind of lemon, bergamot, orange or other citrus fruits. While expression used to be considered a laborious process that could only be done manually using the hands, the advent of savvy technology processes have ensured expression of rinds is now a mechanized process. For home practice, you may experiment with a fruit rind by cutting off a peel segment of washed and dried fruit and pierce this peel with a knife tip. Place over a bowl and carefully squeeze the rind to get drops of essential oil. Preserve your oil by storing in a dark glass bottle and keep in a cool place. This may seem a crude way, but your product is just as fine as any commercially sold essential oil obtained from citrus, and so can be a reliable product when you need to perform aromatherapy.

In a process recently discovered, carbon dioxide carbon dioxide can also be used at low temperatures for the extraction process, resulting in highly fragrant aromas.

Although preferable to solvent extraction, the only caveat with this process, aromatherapists believe, is in the fact that it requires the use of highly expensive equipment to carry out the extraction process successfully. Consequently, the oils obtained are more expensive and may not be easily within reach. Others at dissent with this process say the temperature required for CO_2 extraction is barely high enough for proper distillation of the plant molecules. Hence the essential oils obtained, they posit, should not be used for therapeutic purposes but rather in candles, soaps and room deodorizers.

5% OR 10% OILS

These blends are often associated with costly essential oils, although suppliers ensure they are budget friendly by using career oil to dilute them. It is noteworthy, however, that the stipulated percentage is not to mean the quality of essential oil but its quantity. Hence when bottles are described as containing '5% Rose Absolute in Jojoba,' this means that the bottle contains 95% jojoba oil combined with 30 drops of 1.5ml of pure rose absolute.

FRAGRANCE & PERFUME OILS

Fragrance and perfume oils are synthetically made aromas designed to simulate natural aromas but they are dissimilar to pure essential oils. The scents of fragrance and perfume oils mimic natural scents, bringing qualities of richness, familiarity, endurance and complexity. However, these fragrances are chiefly made to be combined with soaps, perfumes, skincare and hair products as well as in making candles, household cleansers and deodorizers. They are never designed for use in aromatherapy. Common examples of these oils are Black Rose, China Rain, Forest, Vanilla and Lily of the Valley.

HYDROSOLS

Also referred to as hydrolat or flower/floral water, hydrosols are the vapor by- product obtained after a distillation process. They essentially have the same fragrance and benefits of essential oils, and they are usually employed in the making of skin care products that have essential oils. Cosmetically intended flower waters include those made from neroli, chamomile and rose petals.

NEAT

Due to the strong concentration of essentials and the high chance of hurting the skin if applied directly, most essentials come with the warning "Do not apply neat." But there are few exceptions; tea tree and lavender oils can be applied to the skin directly when in combination with career oils.

ORGANIC OILS

Organic essentials are those produced from plants that have not been subjected to synthetic applications or processes. There is often a USDA green and white circular seal on food products certified to be organic; the same seal goes on "organic essential oils." Hence if pesticides and synthetic fertilizers were used on a plant or the plant was processed artificially and has chemical preservatives or additives, the essential oil derived therefrom will not come across as organic.

"Organic" might loosely be connected with words like "chemical-free," "no pesticides," "100% natural," "grown wild," and "all-herbal" among others. However, they are not always to mean they are truly 100% organic. A best practice to ensure safety and authenticity is to look out for the USDA seal on the product or be convinced that the dealer is truly letting you have an organically grown and manufactured product.

Two contrasting groups exist in aromatherapy as regards the superior aroma and benefit, or otherwise, of organic essentials as opposed to non-organic oils. While some believe that essential oils are laden with a significant contaminant load due to being highly concentrated (no substantial scientific backing to this claim though), others hold that an effectively carried out distillation process leaves out any fertilizer or pesticide contaminant and ensures the water, steam or alcohol distilled oils are essentially pure products. The choice of organic oil over non-organic alternatives is absolutely a personal decision. Nonetheless, the immense natural composition and benefits make organic oils get the nod for use in aromatherapy. The only caveat being that they are always more expensive, and probably twice as much, when compared to non-organic options.

How to Choose Essential Oils

As with many popular products, choosing the right essential can be a mazy decision, complicated by the presence of many options and varieties. There are also oodles of fragrances to choose from when looking to douse stress, improve your mood or use for health purposes. The extracts vary in purpose too, due to their components, and so while some are best used as topical creams for reversing scars and acne symptoms, others are first choice stress relievers.

Whatever your reason for cashing in on an essential oil, ensuring that the scent is very appealing is a basic thing to look out for; some essential oils can present pungent smells while others, like those made from citrus, are characteristically flowery in smell. You also want to keep the products some good distance away to prevent triggering reactions like headache; this is especially important if the essential is undiluted. Taking a break in between tests will also help make better decisions as over saturation of smells can impair your judgment of the scents.

Another tripwire to look out for is if your retailer sets a specific price for all essential oils. Considering the fact that some essential oils aren't common and so should be expectedly expensive, stacking essential oils at the same price may be a subtle sign that some of the oils, especially the rare ones, are not original. For example, they may have been subjected to cheaper distillation methods or have undesired by-products in the product packaging.

If oily solvents tend to present challenges or trigger allergic responses, you may consider not going with essential oils diluted using vegetable oil since chances exist of having residues in the final product. A nifty way to go about detecting if your essential was diluted using vegetable oil is to place a tiny drop of it on a paper. If residues are left behind as the drop slides off, you likely have a vegetable oil diluted with essential oil.

Top quality essential oils are excellently pure and shouldn't portend any allergic reactions or dangers when used. Pure essential oils are also first choice for aromatherapists since they are clearly stronger in therapeutic effect than synthetic oils. Essential oils should also stored properly in a dark or navy blue container as this will help to preserve the ingredients. Exposing your product to sun lights sets the recipe for product deterioration and, consequently, loss of activity when used for therapeutic purposes.

3
ESSENTIAL OILS BUYING GUIDE

TOP 10 LISTS

It is believed that over 3000 essential oils exist, and of these, about 300 are therapeutically relevant and routinely used in aromatherapy. Out of these therapeutically beneficially oils, 101 are traded globally. In most cases, every merchant, manufacturer or practitioner has varying "top ten" lists of essential oils, and they are never the same since there are varying determinants to be factored. For example, you may have a "Top 10 Best Selling, " Top 10 Florals," and "Top 10 Recommend" lists of essential oils. So you may decide to go with your own list of Top 10 essential oils based on the needed criteria.

CHOOSING ESSENTIAL OILS

The categorization of essential oils can be done in a number of ways. While some are alphabetical, others may be labeled botanically, chemically, aromatically, according to ailment or some other sort of categorization. There are either positive or negative states for the physical, emotional and mental wellbeing of an individual. And hence, reversing any unwanted health condition demands an equally potent solution.

Essential oils can be labeled as positive or negative in effect, depending on their effect. "Negative" essential oils are calming, relaxing, and sedative or essentially tension reliving in nature. Positive essential oils, on the other hand, are meant to invigorate, rejuvenate, or stimulate the body for a better mood. This method has been used in chapters 6 and 7 to give a list of 24 basic essential oils, all of which are top oils recommended by retailers, aromatherapists, authors and manufacturers.

However, the list is obviously not exhaustive and there are surely many more essential oils you may include, depending on your intended use. The given list is only a good reference point when getting started. Select five oils from the list of "12 Essential Oil Relaxants" and another five from the list of "12 Essential oil stimulants" as may be defined by the condition or use. With that out of the way, visit a store where essential oils can be sniffed and have a feel of the options you want. Anything off is not what you want, so discard such aromas and go for oils that are appealing to your sense of smell. Your essential oils list can be grown in due course as you get to know more about them or based on future needs.

LABELING

Been abreast of labeling when choosing a product, and more so when buying an essential oil, can be a goldmine. Manufacturers may not intentionally be deceptive, but essential oils can be labeled in different ways, making it difficult to identify what option you should go with. You don't necessarily need to be a pro as regards essential oils, but there are a few things to look out for in the labeling before choosing one.

STRAIGHT-FORWARD LABELING:

- Therapeutic Essential Oil
- 100% Pure Essential Oil
- No additives, no pesticides
- First distillation
- Maximum therapeutic benefit
- Undiluted & pure

You may not have the most acute awareness of the nuances in essential oil labeling. However, getting to know the basics can save you time and money when buying a product. For example, a product containing only three drops of lavender oil in 8 ounces of jojoba oil may be labeled as "100% pure essential oil," and that may not be faulted if the product wasn't marketed as "undiluted." First distillations are likely going to be the highest quality you can get, with subsequent distillations being essential oils that are slightly weaker.

DUBIOUS LABELING:

- Rich in essential oil
- Vitamin-enriched oil
- Blend containing pure essential oil
- Extracted from whole plant
- Plant-based oil

Also important in the labeling of essential oils is checking for the plant part that the oil was obtained from. For example, if research establishes that the best essential oil of a plant is only obtainable from its roots, going for a product that contains the "leaf extract" of such plant may not be a great idea. Essential oil obtained from orange blossom flower will hugely be different from that obtained from orange rind as they will come with contrasting properties and hence suitable for therapeutically different benefits. Cashing in on a single essential oil as opposed to pre-mixed remedies or blends is also advisable as: you get to determine the extent of dilution that is suitable for your need, can regulate the nature and intensity of the aroma as well as have a better shelf life since undiluted essential oils last considerably longer.

SHOPPING

Shopping for any material requires due diligence, and essential oils are no exception. With literally endless lists of organic grocery stores, health food stores, cosmetic stores and perfumeries to shop from, ensuring you don't get ripped off takes more than finding a visually appealing website if you decide to purchase online. Getting reliable reviews and samples, if possible, are some ways to nip potential issues in the bud when purchasing an essential oil.

Pricing is another tricky area to consider. You want to compare various outlets for the same product before reaching a decision. Quality rose otto can be sold anywhere from $300 to $700 per 15ml. There are higher priced alternatives, but you only want to buy those when assured of getting the best value for money. Prices may also hinge on the country of origin, for example, Indian sandalwood essential retails at about $150 per ounce or 30ml, while Australian products from the same sandalwood can be sold for $80 per ounce. Shipping costs may be important too if you are cash- strapped. As some big online outlets can offer free shipping on specific orders, consider that before making a purchase.

Product packaging is equally key. Products packaged in black, brown or dark bottles are especially great since constituents will have been adequately protected from the deteriorating effects of sunlight. The presence of oxygen can also affect the color and odor of essential oils. Stored properly, quality essential oils can last anywhere from 6 to 24 months.

4
WAYS TO USE ESSENTIAL OILS

Essential oils are typically used by topical application or inhalation but never by ingestion, except in extreme cases which should, of course, be guided by a licensed physician or medical personnel.

Inhaling an essential oil helps to balance activities in both right and left parts of the brain. It also stimulates the production and distribution of certain hormones to other parts of the body. When applied topically on the skin, essential oils reach the bloodstream and ultimately get to specific parts of the body that the healing is intended. The specificity of essential oils means they are active and best compatible when in contact with specific hormones, parts of the body, or system. Hence, a product may only work best for muscle tissues, some for bone marrows and so on.

Proper Ways to Apply Essential Oils

Essential oils are typically mild and natural in effect, helping users relieve symptoms of stress, sore muscles, mental fatigue and a host of other conditions. But all these are only possible when applied or used properly. Hence improper use can trigger episodes of allergic reactions and other negative side effects. This is common if, for example, an undiluted essential oil is directly applied to the skin. The result of which may include rash, burn, painful sores or some sort of irritation. A common way to prevent these side effects is to dilute such products in cream or non-greasy oil as may be desired. They should additionally be kept away from the reach of children as they would obviously cause more harm on tender skin when applied undiluted.

Essential oils should be prevented from reaching the eyes, nose or ears as they may cause irritation. If topically applied, wearing latex gloves may help prevent them from becoming excessively absorbed on the fingers. Some essential oils are sensitive to the sun, and so shouldn't be used if you will be going sun tanning afterward. Citrus essential oils are classic examples in this category and include oils like grapefruit oil and bergamot oil.

Testing an essential oil on the skin for any adverse reaction can help in choosing the right product. Simply watch out for any negative effects after dabbing a small quantity on the hand and waiting for 24hrs.

INHALATION METHODS

Inhalation is one of few ways essential oils can be used. Apart from being more convenient and easy to use, it also ensures the potency and effectiveness of the essential oil are not lost when used for aromatherapy. Here are a few ways of inhaling the aroma from essential oils.

- Direct sniffing

    This is the fastest and simplest way of inhaling aromas from essential oils. It is done by sniffing from an open vial or wearing a perfume containing the essential oil mixed with a carrier.

- Cupped hands

    For a more intense inhalation, a few drops of the oil can be placed on the palm. The hands are cupped over the nose and the oil inhaled by slowly breathing in slowly and exhaling similarly while ensuring that the mouth is closed.

- Diffusion method

    In Diffusion, arguably the most thorough inhalation method, oil is diffused into the air using diffusers like electrically heated bowl or candle heated pottery bowl. Other options include a vaporizer, nebulizer, wick inhaler, humidifier, room spray, plug-in atomizer with wick refills, pillow or linen sachet, potpourri or even a multi-reed diffuser. Whichever diffusion method you chose to go with, only a few drops of oil in combination with water or steam will be all that's needed to get the desired therapeutic benefits from essential oils.

TOPICAL APPLICATION

The many ways of topically applying essential oils include:

- Full body massage
  Topical application by massaging the full body is the most common way of applying essential oils on the skin. For specific relief from any ailment, the oil massage can be targeted at reflexology points located on the feet and palm soles. The temples are massaged if headache pains are experienced while abdominal problems can be relieved by applying a localized massage to relax muscles involved in digestion.

- Bath water combined with essential oil
  A more leisure approach, essential oil-treated bath water or Jacuzzi helps to ease the body and drives home a relaxing feeling after a full body massage.

- By combining with skin products
  Another way of topically applying essential oils is by combining your chosen oil with a conditioner, shampoo, face cleanser, moisturizer or lotion. This makes a formidable combination that will both drive a blemish free skin while keeping any inflammatory conditions in check.

DILUTING

In dilution, we mean adding specific drops of essential oil, say three to five drops, to one teaspoon of lotion or carrier oil. This ratio should however be further decreased in the case of facial skin care products. For tub water baths, dissolving in vegetable oil, honey and powdered or liquid milk are reliable ways of ensuring the essential oil is dispersed evenly and not collected in one region.

BLENDING

A best practice is to do your research and have a reliable list of three essential oils that will serve your need. Next is to experiment with them to get the perfect recipe containing the right quantities of your chosen oils before finally combining them for your unique blend. The choice of only three essential oils and a carrier or base oil is to ensure any problems can quickly be identified and fixed immediately. Hence, oils can be removed or added one at a time as you get more acquainted with essential oils. A blend of 5 oils, at most, should suffice for therapeutic use.

5
GENERAL SAFETY PRECAUTIONS

The safety precautions included herein are not exhaustive since essential oils have specific characteristics and so have unique precautions of use. More specific safety precautions of selected essential oils have been provided in the next few chapters. For questions or additional concerns, don't hesitate to consult with your physician or professional aromatherapist.

- The gold standard is to avoid using essential oils directly on the skin when they are "neat" or undiluted. However, tea tree and lavender oils are noticeable exceptions to this rule, but of course, only after experimentation on test patches is successful since some individuals with overly sensitive skin can react to both of these oils, even though they are regarded in aromatherapy as the mildest oils.
- Administration of skin patch test is essential before using an essential oil for the first time.
- Essential oils are not to be used orally, except when advised by, and in the presence of a physician or licensed medical practitioner.
- Essential oils should be used away from fire as they are highly flammable
- If contact is made on sensitive parts like the eye, essential oils should be washed off by irrigation using isotonic, sterile, saline solution for about 15 minutes. Persistent reaction or pains should be reported to a healthcare professional.
- Keep all essential oils away from the reach of children.
- Fennel, rosemary and hyssop are reportedly problematic for patients with epilepsy and so should be avoided if you have the condition.
- Young babies and the elderly should take lower doses of essential oils since they are negatively reactive to some,

especially eucalyptus and peppermint, with respiratory problems commonly reported in users belonging to these age bracket. And as mild as they may appear, only minute quantities, for example, one drop in bath water or ½ drop per ounce of carrier oil of both lavender and neroli is usually tolerated.

- Cancer patients may only use essential oils like chamomile, bergamot, ginger, lavender and frankincense in their mild dilutions, while aniseed and fennel should be avoided.
- Individuals undergoing chemotherapy sessions are advised not to use essential oils to avoid adverse effects.
- Persons with high blood pressure should not use peppermint, black pepper, hyssop, clove, sage, rosemary or thyme essential oils.
- Lavender oil should also be avoided by low blood pressure patients.
- Individuals with the tendency to exhibit allergic reactions to nuts should stay away from peanut or almond carrier oils. Better alternatives to be used instead are canola (non-GM), sunflower and safflower oils.
- Women who are pregnant should stay clear of essential oils prior the 18th week of pregnancy. This is even more important if there is a history of miscarriage. Essential oils may however be used in low doses in the second trimester but should be formulated by an expert aromatherapist or health care professional.

6
TWELVE ESSENTIAL OIL RELAXANTS

BERGAMOT

A predominant citrus fruit grown in Calabria, Italy, Bergamot tastes sour but has a surprisingly lemony, sweet rind with a refreshing and mild fragrance. While it has been grown in parts of the United States and South America, Italian Bergamot leads the pack in all ramifications. The green or yellow oil gotten from bergamot has been extensively used in perfumes and colognes as well as in producing Earl Grey tea where it enhances the unique aroma of the drink. Dubbed the "sunny" oil, bergamot is hugely calming but equally energizing and soothing in effect.

This fruit is effective in treating fever and a wide range of skin conditions like psoriasis, eczema, acne, herpes and oily skin. It also works well for cystitis and many urinary tract infections. While a good appetite stimulant, it also helps in shedding weight.

Bergamot's rich anti-depressant benefits ensure it is a handy regimen for anger, anxiety, stress relief or any Seasonal Affective Disorder (SAD).

PRECAUTIONS:
- Not to be used undiluted on the skin or "neat." Bergamot can be applied on the skin when diluted in a lotion, carrier oil or bath water.
- Bergamot is highly sensitive to the sun, and so should not be used within 12 hours before sun exposure to prevent adverse effects. An exception though is 'Bergaptine Free' or 'Bergamot FCF' labeled bergamot oil which poses no skin problems if used before exposure to the sun.

CHAMOMILE

Extracted from white flowers, Chamomile appears deep blue and tastes sweet and fruity with a subtly bitter undertone. Dried chamomile bearing flowers are commonly used in making chamomile tea which has a positively refreshing aromatic aftereffect. Chamomile comes in different varieties, but Roman and German species are particularly high in medicinal value. Its gentle nature means it is one of very few essential oils that can be used during pregnancy as well as for infants and young children.

Oil from chamomile is a useful anti-inflammatory agent that works effectively against symptoms of allergies like eczema and skin problems like blisters and rash. The analgesic property of chamomile guarantees an invaluable solution for migraines, headaches, stomach ache and premenstrual cramping. Chamomile is also sedative, making it great for anxiety, insomnia, mood swings, nervous tension and other emotional imbalances.

PRECAUTION:
- Fresh chamomile oil appears blue, green colors are signs of deterioration and such should not be used.

CLARY SAGE

This tall herb, also called salvia, comes in purple-green and hairy leaves. When steamed, petals of clary sage give off a musky oil that comes with a nutty tone and enhances mood while being deeply revitalizing and relaxing.

Clary sage oil is analgesic in nature, and so makes it an excellent option for menstrual cramps, stomach pains, hot flashes associated with menopause and pains during labor. It is also effective for headaches and migraines and can be used to relieve asthma too. Dermatologically, applying clary sage can help treat conditions like dandruff for a lush and healthy scalp.

The oil is also known to trigger "high" like properties, therefore making it a strong agent for mood problems like depression and anxiety. It helps stimulate creative thinking, promotes restful sleep and can drive improved meditation.

PRECAUTIONS:
- Being a mood enhancing essential oil, clary sage shouldn't be used with alcohol or other recreational drugs.
- Not suitable for pregnant mothers, young children or individuals 18 years and below.

FRANKINCENSE

Native to African and Middle Eastern Countries and India, Frankincense has a milky- white resin that can be steamed to produce a fresh, woody fragrance essential oil with balsamic, smokey tones. Frankincense has a long history and was synonymously used by a number of religions for purification rites over many centuries. Frankincense oil is known to have a calming and rejuvenating effect and has been used for disinfection and perfume fixative purposes. It has a strong dermal property, thus the essential oil is used in skin care to reverse skin conditions like wrinkles, dry and scaly skin, scars, and stretch marks. Frankincense oil has also been used for bronchitis, asthma, sinusitis, coughing spell, sore throat and cold. The robust essential oil was used in a research at the University of Connecticut in 2008 to successfully treat knee osteoarthritis. Frankincense essential oil is considered strongly effective in helping induce slow deep breathing, quashing feelings of fear and promoting overall emotional strength. Nervous tension, nightmares, sadness, stress and anxiety are other uses of the wondrous Frankincense oil.

LAVENDER

Another beneficial plant used in Aromatherapy is Lavender. Lavender oil is gotten from purple flowers of shrubs with green or gray leaves popularly cultivated worldwide. However, those growing in England and France have particularly been highly appreciated. Lavender oil appears colorless to pale yellow-green and has a characteristic floral fragrance. It is mildly sweet with a woody undertone. Lavender's popularity and widespread use have ensured it is dubbed the "Cure-all Oil" or "Queen of Essential Oils." But it is not hard to see why too. The oil works sublimely effective and blends with essences for improved effectiveness. Lavender oil is considered to stimulate the activation of the brain's pineal gland, thereby helping restore body functions and emotions. It's particularly effective in advancing a calming, relaxing and soothing effect. Lavender is routinely used in the production of skin care products, so expect to find this essential oil in creams and soaps as well as perfumes and household cleaners.

It's considerably mild too; it can be used on infants and young children when diluted in lotions or carrier oils. But that's not all if you fancy adding lavender to your top ten list of essential oils. In combination with massage oil or bath water, Lavender is considered a superb analgesic for muscle spasms and headaches. Viral infections, cold, bronchitis and sinus congestion can also be relieved by using Lavender oil.

The terrific oil can be used undiluted on wound and burn surfaces as it mildly speeds up the healing process. Want to better repel insects or treat their bites? How about allergy induced itching and acne? You can give lavender oil a try for these and more. Lavender is also your reliable oil for anger, mood swings, anxiety, insomnia and hyperactivity while the soothing effect ensures relief is in the offing if you are constantly warding off foggy thinking or want to enhance your insight, rationality and quality of meditation.

PRECAUTION:
- While Lavender oil is undoubtedly beneficial, mothers in the first three months of pregnancy are advised to jettison the use of lavender.

MARJORAM
The bushy herb – Marjoram – has dark silver-green leaves and a bundle of small, whitish pink flowers. Expect a colorless and slightly

warm and spicy aroma. Popular uses of Marjoram in Ancient Egypt include perfumes, ointments and flavoring of foods. The essential oil is also called "the great comforter" due to its very powerful sedating benefits.

By dilating the blood vessels, Marjoram finds use in improving circulation and relieving pains including migraine headache, stiff joints, sore muscles, rheumatism and arthritic pains. Digestion problems like flatulence and constipation can also be relieved by taking an abdominal massage session using Marjoram. Stress-induced sexual inactivity can be fixed with this essential oil as it is also an aphrodisiac with a terrific sedating property.

On the emotional end of the spectrum, the oil can help bring back mood downed by grief or loneliness. Insomnia, Obsession (OCD), Hyperactivity (ADD/ADHD) and trauma (PTS) are other conditions that can be reversed by Marjoram oil.

PRECAUTIONS:
- Numbing effects have been reported. Hence, the oil should be used with care. Extended use can cause adverse effects on the senses.
- Not to be used during pregnancy.

NEROLI

Popularly referred to as orange blossoming, Neroli oil, pale yellow in color, comes from the fragrant white flowers of Seville orange. Neroli has a cool floral scent with a characteristically bitter-sweet undertone. It is a popular ingredient used in the production of perfumes and similar cosmetics. A quintessence of purity and innocence, just like its flowers, Neroli is believed to help soothe the evident jitters of a groom or bride. This is due to it's pure, uplifting, calming and slightly hypnotic characteristics. The dazzlingly stunning fragrance is unsurprisingly one of the most expensive essential oils. Neroli oil helps in cell regeneration, so it is a go-to choice for dry and sensitive skin. It helps to tone facial muscles and skin, making it a mainstay in many skin care products and massage oil. Abdominal problems like diarrhea can also be relieved by having a Neroli oil massage.

Professional aromatherapists find this oil top of the list for shock, chronic anxiety and disappointment. Neroli oil is also an effective solution for feelings of despair, depression, hysteria, panic attacks and post-traumatic stress disorder. Rolling back these conditions and enhancing optimism, confidence and initiative driven actions. A mild aphrodisiac, Neroli makes it easier to overcome shyness or anxiety related to sexual activity.

ROSE

Rose is one flower we've all come across. But it's not just its beauty and striking elegance that is captivating. Rose petals are an incredible source of essential that provide numerous benefits. While there are oodles of species of this flower, Damascus, Cabbage or French Rose are exceptionally useful in aromatherapy. A product of water distillation, "Rose otto" is easily the priciest essential oil you can find in the market, selling for around $500 and $1,400 per ounce. You can also cash in on a drop of "Rose otto" between $1.25 to $4.00. The clear to slightly pale yellow oil presents a gentle, light, sweet and spicy aroma. Another option is "Rose Absolute" which distills with alcohol to appear in brown to orange colors with a deep, honeyed aroma that is appreciably stronger than rose otto. In contrast to rose otto, it is not as expensive and can easily be bought at half the price of rose otto. Hence, it is not uncommon to find some aromatherapist prefer rose otto, which they believe is more superior. However, it only comes down to differences in fragrance since the two both have the same therapeutically beneficial properties.

Rose oil finds relevance in many conditions. Like some other essential oils, it is proven beneficial for dry and scaly skin. A massage bath with the oil is also considered particularly effective for women dealing with postpartum depression, premenstrual cramps and menopause. The oil is also an aphrodisiac, and hence can help in reversing sexual anxiety and enhancing confidence instead.

Rose essential oil wards off feelings of sadness, grief or disappointment while fostering a stronger inner spirit. The end result is a comfortable ambiance that radiates inwards and outwards for better expression of love to everyone.

PRECAUTION
- Individuals with a history of miscarriage are advised to stay off this essential oil in the first trimester of pregnancy. However, it can be used without concerns in the second and third trimesters.

SANDALWOOD

The roots and heartwood of sandalwood tree are distilled to get sandalwood oil. The tree itself provides wood that is regarded one of the strongest in the world.

Sandalwood essential oil appears pale to dark yellow and has tremendous longevity, staying rich with a radiant fragrance even after an extended period of time when other essential oils would notably have gone rancid.

The oil has a sweet taste with a woody aroma and spicy touch, providing a harmonizing and balancing psyche effect which has ensured its relevance for spiritual use and meditation for thousands of years. The uplifting fragrance has made it a great choice in making male and female perfumes. Indian varieties of sandalwood are widely cherished. The rarity of sandalwood due to growing extinction have driven the high price of this essential oil. However, Australian sandalwood oil can be gotten far cheaper than Indian alternatives and is also considered satisfactorily good by professional aromatherapists.

Essential oil from sandalwood is characteristically calming and soothing and is the most popular option for conditions like laryngitis and bronchitis. The oil is also appreciably effective for urinary tract and bladder infections and has also helped reverse fluid retention. Sandalwood oil has an astringent property, hence it is used for treating a wide range of scalp conditions. When used in bath water of massage oil, sandalwood promotes a relaxing feeling and helps relieve tension and headache. The benefits also encompass aggression, sadness and obsessive thinking. A strong aphrodisiac, the essential oil can be all that's needed to treat stress and depression induced impotence.

PRECAUTION:
- The essential oil is noticeably strong and shouldn't be directly applied on the skin if undiluted.

SPEARMINT

Spearmint essential oil is produced from the distillation of the herb's pink or lilac colored flowers, the leaves of which are luxuriantly green and can grow to about 3 feet long. The oil, yellowish green in color, has a fresh and mint-like aroma that reminds of peppermint. But it is milder and sweeter than the latter.

Suitable for children, the essential oil is a regular flavor in candy, chewing gum, food and medications due to its sweet and cooling effect. The tea from spearmint can be a superb drink when going to bed. It is believed that Ancient Greeks explored the antiseptic and refreshing benefits of spearmint oil by including it in bath water.

A huge range of conditions can benefit from spearmint essential oil. Some of these are chronic respiratory problems including sinusitis and bronchitis. Chest pains and headache can also be relieved using this oil. Other problems that can be treated using spearmint oil are digestive problems synonymous with spams and tension problems. Thus, an abdominal massage can help relieve flatulence, vomiting, hiccups, constipation, and nausea. Its brightening effect means spearmint has found use as a teeth whitener while enhancing gum tissue health. In combination with facial cleansers, this essential oil can help close pores which would otherwise trigger acne, ensuring that your skin is healthier and uniformly toned. Like many other essential oils, spearmint is refreshingly cool and enhances mood, so you can have it a handy inclusion for mild depression and mental fatigue.

PRECAUTIONS:
- While spearmint is usually present in food flavors and common nonprescription medications, it is not a safe practice to ingest any essential oil, including spearmint oil, without due advice and guidance by a medical practitioner.
- In some cases, spearmint can cause irritations in the eyes. It may also be problematic when used on sensitive skin, even if it was diluted before use.

TEA TREE

This shrub has green to yellow leaves that appear needlelike. The tree's bark is characteristically unique and is usually called paper bark due to its papery and white appearance. The essential oil is gotten from the leaves and twigs and has a pungent and spicy aroma like that of nutmeg. The oil is pale yellow and presents a subtle camphor odor. Tea tree is highly active against many infections caused by bacteria, fungi and viruses, hence making it a formidable product in first-aid ointments. The healing and penetrating effects of tea tree oil radiate physically and emotionally. Due to its highly active nature and gentleness, the oil can be applied undiluted on the skin and used to successfully treat conditions including nail fungus, skin rash, cold sores, athlete's foot, herpes, head lice, insect bites, acne and skin abrasions. Discomforting vaginal infection caused by yeast can also be treated by having warm tea tree baths and frequent abdominal massage when combined with a carrier oil.

With gargling and steam inhalation, tea tree oil can help reverse symptoms of sore throat and cold. It can also be used to enhance resistance to sinusitis, bronchitis and laryngitis. The immune system will benefit from the boosting effects of massage and baths with tea tree oil. This is especially advised when suffering from long-term deleterious illnesses like infectious mononucleosis caused by Epstein - Barr virus.

Shingles pain can be rescinded by applying Tea tree combined with aloe vera gel. The strong, powerful aroma of tea tree helps to clear the mind, counters fatigue and enhances concentration. By promoting confidence and boosting endurance and strength, Tea tree oil lubricates the mind and positions the body for quicker healing.

PRECAUTIONS:
- Should not be used excessively. Bath water with a maximum of drops is just sufficient. 2% in lotion or massage oil should also not present adverse effects.
- Might have irritating effects, especially when applied on sensitive skin.

YLANG-YLANG

Indonesia is home to the large tropical flowers of the Cananga tree from which the essential oil of ylang-ylang is derived. "ylang-ylang" in Malayan translates as "flower of flowers." The essential oil is clear in appearance, pale yellow in color with an exceedingly sweet, almond fragrance and an exotic, balsamic note. The smell is sensationally captivating and sedating, and hence makes ylang-ylang essential oil a mainstay in perfumes and confectioners. The highest grade of the oil is called "ylang- ylang extra," and is usually first choice for use in aromatherapy.

Although ylang-ylang is used for a good number of conditions, high blood pressure, rapid breathing and unusual heart palpitations are where it is prominently used.

Nonetheless, the essential oil is also usually found in skin and hair care products where it is used to treat excessive oiliness. A potent aphrodisiac, an abdominal or groin massage using ylang-ylang can help to reverse frigidity and impotence.

The calming effect makes it a good stress reliever. The essential oil can be used to overcome feelings of anger, frustration, sadness and more intense emotional problems like post-traumatic stress. By helping promote inner tranquillity and peace, ylang-ylang helps conscious meditation and fosters better creative thinking. Adding a few drops of the essential oil in bath water will expectedly enhance mood and relax the mind, both of which are invaluable in treating sleep disorders like insomnia.

PRECAUTIONS:

- To be used only in small amounts. Extensive use over a long period may trigger nausea and headaches. Negative side effects can, however, be prevented by blending ylang-ylang with bergamot or neroli.

7
THE BASIC ESSENTIAL OILS

BASIL

Basil is an aromatic herb with tiny white flowers and yellow-green leaves. Also called "holy basil" or "sweet basil," the essential oil from the herb is pale yellow in color with a sweet, light mint aroma and fruity, spicy fragrance. Basil oil may come across as similar to rosemary oil, but it is noticeably more subtle than the latter. It is mildly stimulating and powers the senses for better stamina. Indians believe the basil herb helps to protect the spirits and homes of inhabitants, hence it is popularly grown in India as a houseplant.

In combination with a massage oil, basil acts a strong anti-spasmodic, helping relieving tensions in the muscle and promoting digestion by relieving digestive spasms. These benefits make the oil of basil a viable product for women experiencing menstrual cramps or chest congestion. Physical exhaustion caused by long-term debilitating illnesses can be remedied using basil oil. Hence it is a perfect springboard when a good burst of energy is needed.

By enhancing quick thinking, basil oil can stimulate better mental awareness and drive good decision making. It is a veritable essential oil for fighting depression, psychic exhaustion or ennui and lethargic feelings. Basil oil also helps to decongest the mind before meditation

PRECAUTIONS:
- Not to be used during pregnancy or by individuals with hypersensitive skin.
- Unsuitable for users under 16.
- Should be used in small quantities not exceeding 2% (6 drops to 1/2 oz) of lotion or carrier oil.
- Extended use and undiluted application can cause adverse effects.

CINNAMON LEAF

Cinnamon essential oil is gotten from leaves of the cinnamon tree. While Cinnamon bark has a strong fragrance and produces a brown/dark-red essential oil, it is peculiarly irritating on the skin, and obviously wouldn't come as first choice for use in aromatherapy. However, cinnamon leaf-derived essential oil is greatly aromatic and has a sweet and spicy fragrance that is slightly peppery and clove-like, except it is sharper and stronger.

Cinnamon is popularly used as a flavor in cooking and also finds huge relevance in medicine. The essential oil obtained from the leaf is inspiring and exhilarating.

Cinnamon oil is sublime for cold and bacterial infections when used in a vaporizer or diffuser. It also helps expedites recovery when down with a respiratory illness.

Cinnamon, used in abdominal massage, can reverse symptoms of poor digestion, flatulence and flu-like symptoms. The oil is also helpful in relieving stiffness or arthritic pains when used for massage on spines and joints. It can help normalize emotional imbalance, thus it is a great essential oil to quash feelings of sadness and isolation while providing the needed spark for lethargic conditions.

PRECAUTIONS:
- Essential oil of cinnamon leaf should not be used by individuals with sensitive skin.
- Best used in minute quantities. Maximum of 3 drops in bath water, or ½ oz. in lotion or massage oil.

CLOVE BUD

This evergreen is not just popular for producing purple berries and fragrant red flowers; from the center of its blossoms are rose-pink buds that can be dried under the sun and processed by distillation to give the clove essential oil which comes with a fresh and spicy fragrance that mimics cinnamon but different in being less intense or strong.

The oil is pale yellow in appearance and has routinely been an integral part of perfumes, food and medicine for thousands of years in a rich history that dates back to ancient China, Egypt and Rome. The aroma of clove is described as intriguing, mysterious, and mildly stimulating. Clove is therefore a very warming analgesic with a comforting and soothing effect. These benefits mean clove oil provides reliable help in remedying toothache pain when applied on aching tooth or gum tissue. It also works as a breath freshener and works well for muscle ache and joint stiffness that come with arthritis and rheumatism. Indigestion, clove oil enhances appetite and provides solution for indigestion, flatulence and nausea. It is incredibly awesome for illness-induced emotional negativity and generally helps to energize and revitalize the mind for a fulfilling day.

PRECAUTIONS:
- Should not be used on dry or sensitive skin.
- Not to be used excessively to prevent side effects. Bath water should not contain more than three drops of clove oil while massage oil and lotions are best combined with ½ ounce of the oil.

EUCALYPTUS

Eucalyptus is extremely diverse with more than seven hundred species known. However, only about twenty of these are important in aromatherapy, with each having slight differences. The evergreen eucalyptus tree can grow as high as 30 meters, producing dark green leaves wherefrom the essential oil is obtained. The oil has a characteristically sharp aroma, with a woody and balsamic tone. Eucalyptus is widely invigorating and piercing and is among a few essential oils with a consistently increasing potency as it ages. Eucalyptus is easily a go-to choice when treating colds, sinusitis or bronchitis, regardless of if it's a viral, bacterial or fungal infection. It can be used via steam inhalation to clear respiratory problems while treating headache, sore throat and neuralgia.

Being a potent essential oil against bacteria, it is used as a deodorizer and disinfectant in rooms when in a diffuser or vaporizer. Eucalyptus essential oil is also a great insect repellant and works well in treating insect bites. In bath water, the oil can reverse symptoms of rashes and shingles, while blending with bergamot is an effective solution for cold sores and herpes.

The invigorating and purifying feature means it takes away emotional and mental exhaustion successfully. "lemon eucalyptus" presents a powerful fragrance that can help promote mental agility and concentration during tasks and also helps to clear the mind, allowing for effective sessions when meditating or praying.

GERANIUM

No essential oil can be gotten from ornamental garden geranium. Additionally, only one out of over seven hundred known geranium varieties is relevant in aromatherapy. The whole geranium plant including the stalls, hairy serrated leaves, pink to magenta or red clusters of florets are needed to obtain an essential oil, the fragrance of which is lemon like and herbal with a reminiscent of rose. The light green essential oil is however cheaper than rose oil and is often present in perfumes to make rose oil more effective. The oil has an aroma that provides a harmonizing, refreshing and uplifting effect while fueling increased sense of stability and security.

By stimulating the adrenal cortex, geranium is known to help reverse hormonal imbalance that may present varying problems in women with menopausal symptoms and menstrual cramps. Geranium also has an antiseptic property that makes it invaluable for lymph detoxification or aiding minor wounds in the flesh. It's beautification effects is hinged on regulating skin glands and stalling overproduction of oil, both of which are actively problematic, causing acne and other skin problems.

Geranium helps to promote better circulation that can be helpful in the optimal functioning of the urinary system. Used in massage oil, geranium can be routinely used to reduce cellulite. It can help repel insects and works effectively as a room freshener. Germanium oil in considerably emotionally beneficially and helps to ward off depression, mood swings, anxiety and nervousness as well as stress and fatigue.

JASMINE

A flowering shrub, Jasmine has nice green leaves and white blossoms from which the essential oil is derived by solvent extraction to give a "Jasmine absolute" – the only form of jasmine essential oil. The dark orange colored oil has a strong fragrance with a sweet, honey undertone. But it does take a lot of jasmine flowers to produce a decent amount of Jasmine absolute. About one thousand pounds of jasmine flowers yield less than 4.5 grams of the absolute. So, it is understandably one of the most expensive oils on the market. Jasmine gives off its strongest scent at night, and hence it is popularly dubbed the "queen of the night." The oil is mildly hypnotic but surely euphoric, liberating, and assuredly revitalizing. Little wonder it goes as a first choice perfume for many users.

But that's not all there is about Jasmine. Apart from scenting well and holding strong in perfumes, it also works excellently in the skin department by helping rejuvenate and giving a vibrant look. Added to warm water, Jasmine absolute can be used to effectively combat joint stiffness, muscle spasm and sustained episodes of sprained ligaments. It's also reproductively beneficial for both gender, as it can be used in back or abdominal massage to reduce labor pains and reduce discomforts that may occur when the prostate gland becomes enlarged. A strong aphrodisiac effect positions it to help stir vigor and stimulate passions for a happier family.

The solidly stimulating nature makes it a reliable antidepressant that can bring back the confidence and good sense of judgment needed for individuals dealing with lethargy and indecision problems. Hence, it thwarts pessimism, annihilates fear and rules out paranoia, the end result being a more rounded and elevated thinking with enhanced positive emotions.

LEMON

The rind of lemon fruit produces the essential oil when cold pressed. Lemon essential oil appears yellowish green but differs from that of "lemon-petitgrain," "lemon balm" or "lemongrass," all of which have different aromatherapy benefits due to their characteristic properties. Lemon oil gives off a sweet scent that reminds of fresh lemon rind, however, it is stronger and longer lasting. Lemon oil is often present perfume, personal care products as well as in household cleaners. It also has relevance in medicine and is a popular addition in food flavoring. Lemon oil comes with a refreshing, invigoration and purifying aroma.

The essential oil is ideal for use in detoxifying all of the respiratory, circulatory and lymphatic systems. It is also a good wound cleanser and can be used to treat sore throat and colds due to its antibacterial properties. An acid neutralizer, lemon oil is additionally great for gout and neutralizes excessively acidic stomach. It can as well be used for rheumatism. Included in skin care products, lemon works to reverse dull and oily skin, while clearing dark spots and varicose veins. Used in addition to shampoo or to rinse hair after a wash, lemon is known to enhance a crisp and dazzling sheen. Bathing in lemon oil can aid recovery from mental fatigue or help to regain vigor after sustained exhaustion from physical activity. Lemon oil enhances fast decision making and rids the mind of anything that impedes concentration, thereby making it an ideal use before mediation.

PRECAUTIONS:
- Lemon oil is particularly sensitive to light, and so should not be applied 24hours before sun exposure
- To be avoided by individuals with sensitive skin.
- Should be used minimally. Not more than three drops in bath water. Massage oil or lotion should not contain more than ½ ounce of lemon oil.

PATCHOULI

Leaves of Patchouli are large, hair and soft. To get Patchouli essential oil, the leaves are first dried and subsequently fermented for a number of days before distillation. This ends with the production of dark orange essential oil whose fragrance is characteristically spicy and wood, with a smoky and balsamic presence. A strong agent used in perfumes, patchouli is also a good deodorizer and also employed to repel moth in carpeting and woven fabrics. The oil is aphrodisiac too, and so both balances and rejuvenates sensual vigor.

A number of skin anomalies can be reversed by applying patchouli essential oil. Some of these conditions include oily skin, dermatitis, dandruff and athlete foot. It particularly helps in skin renewal and helps conceal scar with its regenerative properties.

A great insect repellant, patchouli oil can be useful in treating snake bites too. The essential oil can help deal with pertinent sexual problems including male impotence and frigidity in females.

The emotional benefits make it excellent for anxiety, anger, nervousness and other emotional imbalances. Negative thoughts can ignite depressive moods and confusion can lead to extended vacillation and procrastination, however, they can also be effectively reversed by Patchouli. It is also used to remedy episodic daydreaming and withdrawal problems from hard drugs like tobacco.

PEPPERMINT

The peppermint plant produces flowering tops and downy leaves from which the famous peppermint oil is distilled. The oil is virtually colorless and has a fresh and penetrating smell. The history of peppermint dates back to thousands of years ago when it was popularly explored in ancient Greece and Egypt. This hasn't affected its distribution today, though, as it has gained massive popularity the world over, and is commonly used in food flavoring, candy, gum and in nonprescription drugs. The characteristic pungent aroma comes from menthol, which is predominantly present in amounts ranging from 50% to 80%. Peppermint is highly refreshing, energizing and gives a soothing feel. It has been widely used to help relieve headaches due to its analgesic properties.

A number of digestive problems also respond well to abdominal massage with peppermint oil. Some of these conditions include diarrhea, irritable bowel syndrome, constipation, flatulence, motion sickness, colon spasm and nausea. Carrier oil dilution and application on forehead, temples and neck can help douse migraine pains. Arthritic pains, leg spasm, muscle ache and menstrual cramps can as well be improved with a peppermint massage.

The essential oil can be used as an expectorant or decongestant by massaging on the chest to relieve bronchitis, colds, cough, asthma and sinusitis. Peppermint oil is also reliably antiviral, helping clear herpes and influenza. Fungal yeast and athlete foot infections can also benefit from Peppermint oil. When used as an antiseptic, the essential oil can work to prevent tooth decay, bad breath and gum disease. Inhaled peppermint oil enhances alertness, improves mental clarity and ensures concentration is at its peak. Hence, peppermint fights mental fatigue as well as feelings of apathy and insecurity.

PRECAUTIONS:
- Allergic reactions might be experienced when used on sensitive skin. Thus, it should never be used neat, but in combination with a lotion, carrier oil or bath water.
- Peppermint should not be used for children aged less than five years as chances of adverse reactions to menthol is likely.

PINE NEEDLE

Scotch pine may be popularly recognized by its unique red bark, it also has cones, branches and needle-like leaves from which its essential oil is derived. The pine needles are however the most preferred source for producing the essential oil for aromatherapy use. The clear oil produced smells fresh, with a balsamic fragrance and subtle feel of turpentine. The oil derived from pine has been hugely included in cleansers, soaps, and deodorants alike due to its strong antiseptic properties. A sauna bath ensures its energizing and invigorating effects are fully derived.

The essential oil is the most ideal for making lungs phlegm free. It also has additional respiratory benefits that make it ideal for conditions like sinusitis, colds, hay fever and bronchitis. It is strong against a host of other viral and bacterial infections. In vaporizer, pine oil can bring breathing relief asthma patients while disinfecting the air too.

In massage lotion, pine oil can help treat injuries developed from sports like muscle strain due to excessive exertion and sprains. Bathing with pine oil is believed to help clear cystitis and also gently stimulate and revive weak bladder or kidney function by providing diuretic benefits. It is also a worthy inclusion when treating cellulite with massage.

Pine essential oil helps to relieve symptoms of fatigue as well as mental exhaustion occasioned by tension and irritability. An air diffusion of pine oil brings an aura of confidence, forgiveness and takes away guilt feelings, providing an improved ambiance suitable for meditation.

PRECAUTION:
- Can cause skin irritation even when diluted, especially on individuals with sensitive skin.

ROSEMARY

Essential oil can be derived from the blue flowers of the Rosemary shrub. The resulting colorless and thin oil presents a herbaceous aroma with a tinge of camphor and balsam, ensuring that rosemary has a fresh, medicinal odor. Rosemary is historically considered to help create a form or protection against negative energy and emotions. Consequently, it is used in funerals and weddings for this purpose. It is however commercially used in the preparation of skin care products.

As with all essential oils, loads of benefits abound using rosemary oil. For starters, few drops of the oil can be added in conditioner, shampoo or rinse water to help better stimulation of the scalp, and thus helps to keep off dandruff and promote stronger and better hair growth. In facials, rosemary oil is characteristically revitalizing and rejuvenating, ensuring that dull skin is quickly brought back to life. Going for a full body massage with rosemary oil will help stimulate improved circulation and controlled stiffening on the joints, thereby fighting muscle aches, neuralgia, spasm, arthritis, gout and rheumatism.

The oil is great for use in preventing airborne infection when diffused into the air. Rosemary is considered the foremost essential oil when looking to maintain and improve brain function as it enhances mental stability, increases emotional strength and helps to recover from emotional stress, confusion and general negativity usually experienced with a poor mental balance. It also enhances memory and thus easily tops the chart for students and writers as it helps better intuitive vision, enhances creative thinking and declutters the mind of any impediment to free-flowing mental energy. Rosemary oil is also considered to aid practical thinking and facilitates a better approach when solving emotional, physical and spiritual problems. It is another invaluable essential to fully focus the mind before going on meditation.

PRECAUTION:
- Not to be used during pregnancy or by patients suffering from fever or epilepsy

THYME
Essential oil of this bushy shrub is extracted from its leaves and white top flowers. Over 150 species of thyme are known, the most powerful of which is "red thyme" that has a brown-red or orange color. Red thyme is best applied for use in aromatherapy by air diffusion as it has a high phenol concentration which could cause skin irritation if used otherwise. However, there is subtler variety in

"thyme linalool" which is a thin, pale yellow liquid that can be used on the skin after diluting in a bath water or carrier oil.

A multi-distillation of red thyme called "white thyme essential oil" can be purchased from some manufacturers and is regarded to be more skin friendly.

Whichever the variety, all thyme varieties seem to have identical smells with red thyme being particularly most pungent. Red thyme also has a sweet, spicy and subtly medicinal aroma. Oil from thyme was chiefly used in ancient civilizations of Rome, Egypt and Greece. The oil was essentially used in baths, massage oil, burners, disinfectant and general atmospheric fragrance due to its purifying, energizing, re- balancing and strengthening characteristics.

Thyme oil is also important in fighting bacterial and viral infection. Additionally, it stimulates white blood cells production and consequently makes the immune system more resistant to infections, preventing it from sore throat, colds and influenza.

By enhancing production of red blood cells, thyme oil ensures oxygen is distributed faster to all parts of the body, thereby making the body refreshed and reinvigorated. The oil is helpful in enhancing appetite which usually dips in individuals who are ill. Thyme oil is used to aid digestion and solve constipation problems. The ripple effect is a terrifically energized body and a strongly balanced system. Lost stamina due to fatigue and male impotence and sexual frigidity can all be reversed too.

PRECAUTIONS:
- Thyme has many varieties, however, they shouldn't all be used during pregnancy and also by individuals who have problems with high blood pressure.
- Red thyme should not be used in any case as a massage oil or added in bath water. It is also best avoided for children.

With that, we have come to the end of this book. I want to thank you for choosing this book.

Now that you have come to the end of this book, we would first like to express our gratitude for choosing this particular source and taking the time to read through it. All the information here was well researched and put together in a way to help you understand the essential oils as easily as possible.

We hope you found it useful and you can now use it as a guide anytime you want. You may also want to recommend it to any family or friends that you think might find it useful as well.

MASSAGE THERAPY

A Comprehensive Guide with Secret Tips and Benefits of Massage Therapy

© Copyright 2018 by Jessica Thompson - All rights reserved.

The following eBook is reproduced below with the goal of providing information that is as accurate and reliable as possible. Regardless, purchasing this eBook can be seen as consent to the fact that both the publisher and the author of this book are in no way experts on the topics discussed within and that any recommendations or suggestions that are made herein are for entertainment purposes only. Professionals should be consulted as needed prior to undertaking any of the action endorsed herein.

This declaration is deemed fair and valid by both the American Bar Association and the Committee of Publishers Association and is legally binding throughout the United States.

Furthermore, the transmission, duplication or reproduction of any of the following work including specific information will be considered an illegal act irrespective of if it is done electronically or in print. This extends to creating a secondary or tertiary copy of the work or a recorded copy and is only allowed with an expressed written consent from the Publisher. All additional rights reserved.

The information in the following pages is broadly considered to be truthful and accurate account of facts, and as such any inattention, use or misuse of the information in question by the reader will render any resulting actions solely under their purview. There are no scenarios in which the publisher or the original author of this work can be in any fashion deemed liable for any hardship or damages that may befall them after undertaking information described herein.

Additionally, the information in the following pages is intended only for informational purposes and should thus be thought of as universal. As befitting its nature, it is presented without assurance regarding its prolonged validity or interim quality. Trademarks that are mentioned are done without written consent and can in no way be considered an endorsement from the trademark holder.

CONTENTS

INTRODUCTION 56

1 THE HISTORY OF MASSAGE 59

2 PURPOSE AND BENEFITS OF MASSAGE THERAPY 65

3 EDUCATION AND TRAINING 70

4 BASIC TYPES: EASTERN VERSUS WESTERN; TRADITIONAL VERSUS MODERN ECLECTIC 74

5 COMMON TYPES OF MASSAGE THERAPY 90

6 OTHER TYPES OF MASSAGE THERAPY: EASTERN 97

7 OTHER TYPES OF MASSAGE THERAPY: WESTERN............. 100

8 TERMINOLOGY 103

CONCLUSION 111

INTRODUCTION

With stressful routines and little to no down times in between tasks, stress dousers have become mainstream in today's world. And over the years, a number of therapies and medications have been used for this purpose. One such common method is Massage therapy which has, over the last ten years, gone on to become one of the most popular treatments worldwide.

The rapid rise in massage therapy has expectedly seen an astronomical rise in the demand for massage therapists the world over. Whether for babies, children, the elderly in ICUs or as part of an integrated medical treatment, massage centers are no longer exclusively found in spas and massage parlors as used to be the case. It has also been substantially used for the management of conditions in cancer patients and HIV sufferers. Hence, massage is now an integral part of a wide range of facilities in the healthcare industry. But that's not all. In the world of sports, massage has slowly gained prominence too, so much so that it features in Olympics, with athletes from all around the world looking to ramp up their training with a healthy massage session before a race.

While the benefits of massage therapy have not gone unnoticed, what does massage really mean? The term "massage" has varied over time, with different meanings attributed to it, and as such, there is no unanimous definition for this word. For example, in 1886, *Thomas's Medical Dictionary of 1886* simply stated it as:

"Massage, from the Greek, meaning to knead. Signifying the act of shampooing."

But that was only the beginning, and a few years later, in 1994, a more in-depth definition was given by Doctor Axel V. Grafstrom who defined massage in *A Text- book of Mechano-Therapy* as:

"By massage, we mean a series of passive movements on the patient's body, performed by the operator for the purpose of aiding nature to restore health. These passive movements are friction, kneading, percussion, stretching, pressure, vibration, and stroking."

This definition was widely accepted and massage crept into the 20th century without losing its meaning. However, in 1970, massage was further defined by a standard dictionary to mean a: "manual or mechanic manipulation of parts of the body as through rubbing, kneading, slapping or the like, used to promote circulation, relax muscles, etc."

The Encarta Dictionary provides an online definition of massage, wherein it is defined as:

"a treatment that involves rubbing or kneading the muscles, either for medical or therapeutic purposes or simply as an aid to relaxation."

However, there are many other ways of characterization based on type or method. While some consider massage traditional, others consider it a modern form of relaxing treatment. There are also Asian and Western or Oriental versions too.

With many different types and parameters to be considered, a plethora of definitions hold true for massage therapy. But basically, massage involves the use of contact by one person as a treatment therapy to another.

Massage is carried out manually by kneading, rubbing, stroking, compressing or making some other sort of manipulation on the flesh. In most cases, massage is a pleasure to relish. Massage's powerful relevance means it is a reliable way to treat pains or rehabilitate injuries. It is also generally used to improve health and awareness as well as make athletes recover faster from muscular fatigue after a competition.

While it has gained a reputation for being used for slightly "unsavory" purposes, massage art and skills are hugely relevant today as it was in the past for medical, psychological and emotional treatment. Massage therapy therefore helps individuals to recover from injury or act as a preventive measure e.g. in sports massage.

Being a therapeutic, curative, preventive, or enabling type of medical treatment, massage therapy can be solely employed or used in confluence with other types of treatment regimens. Hence, it can be used in consonance with alternative or traditional therapies to become part of what is referred to as Complementary and Alternative Medicine (CAS).

In the next chapters, we will find out more about the intricacies and nuances of Massage Therapy. The benefits, purposes, training, terminologies used and types as well as the varying techniques and approaches commonly adopted in massage practice. Whether aromatherapy massage or Trigger Point Massage sounds more appealing, find out all you need to know about these and more in this e-book.

1
The History of Massage

Massage has a long history that dates back to the ancient past, with overwhelming oral and written records of its practice among civilizations we've come to know today.

ANCIENT MASSAGE

From the Chinese to the Romans, the Greeks, the Hindus and the Egyptians, many records abound of the tremendous use of massage in the age-old past as a complementary or key part of medical treatment. Egyptian history of massage is pretty evident in its tomb paintings that showed individuals on massage session. It is also believed that the Chinese, around 3000 BC, incorporated massage it into its general health and fitness program. One reference indicating the adoption of massage therapy by the Chinese is *The Yellow Emperor's Classic of Internal Medicine* or Huang Ti Nei Ching Su Wen (ca. 2,700 B.C.) which notes: "When the body is frequently startled and frightened, the circulation in the veins and arteries ceases, and disease arises from numbness and the lack of sensation. In order to cure this one uses massage and medicines prepared from the lees of wine." Some recommendations proffered by the book for the treatment of chills, paralysis and fever include: "breathing exercises, massage of skin and flesh, and exercises of hands and feet"

Hindu writings in 1800 B.C. further indicated that massage therapy was used in a confluence of other treatment for conditions like fatigue, weight loss and improving sleep. These writings also informed the use of massage as a way of improving relaxation. Classical Greece ultimately gives us a more in-depth knowledge of the use of massage in the age-old past.

ANCIENT GREEK MASSAGE

Anatripsis in the Greek word for massage. The use of massage by Greeks was extensively for problems related to muscle pain, fatigue and similar conditions among soldiers. It was adopted since pain and tension were found to be considerably eased by undergoing a massage session during training. The Greek also employed massage in sports, with athletes leveraging it before and after tournaments. However, the first Greek physician to use massage as a form of medical treatment was Herodicus who believed that it helped increase longevity. Herodicus combined massage with oils and herbs in his administration of massage as a form of medical treatment.

This was before one of his students Hippocrates (460 – 380 B.C.) who was dubbed the "Father of Medicine," claimed that massage was significantly beneficial for the improvement of joints and enhancement of muscle tone. Hippocrates considered the heart to be the best place to carry out massage.

There were several mentions of massage in the writings of Hippocrates. Some of his most quoted references regarding massage are in his books "On articulations and "On surgery." In the former, Hippocrates states "The physician must be experienced in many things, but assuredly in rubbing (anatripsis), for things which have the same name have not always the same effects. For rubbing a joint that is too loose, and loosen a joint that is too rigid." (9), while he posits "Anatripsis [massage or rubbing] can relax, brace, incarnate, attenuate: hard anatripsis braces, soft anatripsis relaxes while much anatripsis attenuates and moderate rubbing thickens" in the latter (17).

ROMAN MASSAGE

The Romans were another civilization that followed in the use of massage therapy for many health benefits. "Frictus" which translates as "a rubbing" is the Roman word for massage. It is historically believed that prominent Romans including Pliney and Julius Caesar received some form of massage therapy. While Julius Caesar primarily underwent massage to serve as a relief from headaches and neuralgia, Pliny, on the other hand, employed massage for asthma.

Roman physician Aulus Cornelius Celsus (ca 25BC – ca 50 A.D.) also practised massage, and denoted its importance in his works "De Medicina." The 8 volume set came with a number of volumes that extensively discussed the typology, use, and methods of massage or rubbing. Aulus also posited that massage could provide healing for paralytic patients as well as relieve headaches. Another physician by the name Galen who served both Septmus Severus and Marcus Aurelius further emphasized the useful effects of massage in many medical publications.

MASSAGE IN DAYS OF YORE

After the Roman Empire, there was a noticeable downturn in the practice of massage therapy or similar medical procedures. This was due, in part, to the fact that the medieval times or Dark Ages didn't make concerted efforts at exploring the usefulness of massage. There was also the fact that massage demanded the contact of hand to flesh, a procedure that was considered largely inappropriate and overly sensual for the religiously inclined world of that time. However, this trend was not the case in the Middle East and a host of non-European countries.

A noteworthy contributor in the field of massage therapy for medical purposes was Avicenna (980-1037), a Persian scholar whose real name is Ali al-Husayn Abd Allah Ibn Sinna. Avicenna authored many works of medical relevance and also wrote books on poetry, philosophy and theology. In his words, massage was intended "to disperse the effete matters found in the muscles and not expelled by exercise."

Following the low acceptance of massage in The Middle Ages, the medical regained popularity in the Renaissance period, especially among royal households that reigned that time. Noticeably, in the 16th century, French barber-surgeon Ambroise Paré (1510 – 1590) adopted massage in his practice of medicine and ultimately became the official surgeon for 4 kings including Francis II, Henry II, Henry III and Charles IX. Ambriose works in massage and other fields of medicine ensured the art and science of massage were reinvigorated.

In ensuing years, massage became more popular through the 16th century. Although little advances were made to understand the theory or form of the medical therapy. The greatest achievement of massage therapy, and one which set the tone for the formation of present-day massage therapy, came in the 1700s. This reign was supercharged extensively by two men - John Grosvenor (1742-1823) and Per Henrik Ling (1776-1839).

THE 1800S TO 1900S

Swedish born Per Henrik Ling was a doctor, poet and educator who founded a gymnastics training program that had massage as an integral component. Henrik Ling founded the Royal Gymnastics Central Institute in Stockholm in 1813. His method of medical gymnastics was referred to as the Swedish Movement Cure.

Much of Ling's techniques were reliant on Turk's, but also included parts of Egyptian, Chinese, Roman and Greek massage techniques. Ling's creation soon became called the Swedish Gymnastic Movement System or Swedish Movement System, gaining the misnomer "Swedish Massage" in later years.

As Ling began working on making massage a vital component of healthy lifestyle, Grosvenor wrote on the substantial use of massage in medical treatment and felt massage therapy was a veritable tool in solving a myriad of medical problems including muscle pains, stiff joint pains, gout and rheumatism.

Further contribution to massage therapy came in the 19th century when Johan Georg Mezger (1839-1909), a Dutch doctor, provided the concluding steps to Ling's system and gave the French names used in the now called Swedish Massage. This was particularly important given the fact that Ling didn't provide terminologies for the techniques he employed in his form of massage therapy. By applying French names to key massage strokes, Swedish Massage was now synonymous with terminologies including petrissage, effleurage, tapotement and friction.

Massage soon became introduced into the United States by two brothers George Henry Taylor (1821-1826) and Charles Fayette Taylor (1826-1899). Although they were both physicians, they also got invaluable contributions from Dr S. Weir Mitchell and Dr Douglas Graham from Philadelphia and Boston respectively. Graham was the brain behind several articles on massage and is also credited to have published one of the earliest books on massage in 1884. His work *Recent Developments in Massage* was released in 1893.

As the century waned down, creeping into the 20th century, there were further developments in the field of massage, making it become an increasingly respected form of medical treatment. In 1895, John Harvey Kellogg (1852-1943) employed hydrotherapy and massage as a form of treatment, publishing the treatise *The Art of Massage*.

20TH CENTURY MASSAGE

Following Harvey's work were a number of developments in massage therapy in the 20th century. Sigmund Freud noticeably used massage therapy while treating hysteria, and before the turn of the century, Sir William Bennet advanced the cause of massage by establishing a massage department at St. George's Hospital in London, England in 1899. A massage department was also run at St Thomas's Hospital in London until 1934.

As the 20th century progressed, treatments employing massage became widely accepted for a number conditions and by the end of WWI, in 1918, Kurre W. Ostrom had published his book on Swedish Massage. The popularity of massage wasn't going without new modifications and introductions to its types of systems, and this happened when Jiro Mura introduced Jin shin jyutsu - regarded the Japanese form of massage. Mary Lino Murmeister then made this new introduction public to Americans in the 1960s. Janet Travel afterwards dived deeper into Trigger Point Massage in the 1950s and went on, together with David Simons, to publish her own manual in 1983. In 1963, Ida Pauline Rolf (1896-1979) published a work on Structural Integration (SI) which created and promoted a form of massage referred to as Rolfing. Another massage stalwart of the 20th century was Francis Tappan (1915- 1999) who published her work together with Elizabeth Wood and Gertrude Beard.

The much celebrated and classic textbook *Massage: Principles and Techniques* has since gone on to become a handy tool in the study of massage since it was first published in 1964.

MASSAGE TODAY

Massage now remains a household name and an activity relished by many individuals the world over today. The varying forms and techniques now employed for massage therapy have propelled the art to regain its relevance and high esteem in the field of health care, and the momentum doesn't seem to be waning anytime soon with many people cashing in on one form of massage session or the other.

2
PURPOSE AND BENEFITS OF MASSAGE THERAPY

Massage may popularly be used for relaxation purposes, however there are many more benefits that come with a massage therapy, making it become a reliable way of supercharging a healthy lifestyle. It is even more alluring considering the fact that massage therapy is not exclusively designed to benefit individuals of a certain age bracket, gender or race. The effect of touch is simply terrific, and massage therapy takes it to a whole new level by giving a comfortable feeling while delivering the trust therapeutic touch you need to ward off many conditions.

The application of massage therapy is dependent on the part of the body needing attention, and thus massage therapy comes in varying types. For example, sports massage is focused more on the general body in contrast to ailment driven massage that affects a part of the body. Whichever the type you decide to go for, or the practitioner carrying out the session, there is almost always one goal - helping improve the overall quality of health.

PURPOSES OF MASSAGE THERAPY

While the list of conditions and purposes of massage therapy may seem endless, the main purpose of massage therapy can be linked to one or more of the following:

1. To douse stress and reduce anxiety.

2. For relaxation of tense joints and muscles.

3. Stimulation of the body's circulatory system for enhanced efficiency of all body parts.

4. Improve the response of the immune system.

5. Hasten recovery from an illness.

6. Promote better quality of general health.

7. Eliminate or rescind symptoms of chronic and acute pains.

8. Enhance optimum health by improving homeostasis.

BENEFITS

Massage Therapy serves a number of purposes and consequently brings many benefits to individuals. The benefits of massage have been solidly backed by research. While many more findings are needed to validate data and claims, the National Institutes of Health provide give credence to many benefits of massage therapy, some of which include:

1. Increase in weight gain when infants exposed to the HIV virus undergo the therapy.

2. Faster recovery in patients who undergo abdominal surgery.

3. Benefits to hypertensive individuals by helping decrease blood pressure.

4. Improving symptoms of headaches and migraines.

Concerted efforts are yielding positive answers to questions regarding the benefits of Massage Therapy for a host of other conditions including:

1. Controlling indigestion

2. Regulating high blood pressure

3. As painkillers by their effect of releasing endorphins

4. Hormonal benefits

5. Enhancing blood circulation

6. Promoting more flexible muscles by enhancing the range of motion

7. Controlling swelling in the joints and muscles

8. Controlling scar formation

9. Benefits in minimizing pregnancy discomfort

10. Introducing essential oils into the skin

11. Providing an alternative source to conventional pain management systems.

HOW MASSAGE THERAPY WORKS

A number of activities and processes are activated when a massage session is administered. These processes affect the overall body systems, and effectively so when applied by an expert practitioner. Good therapeutic massage techniques are effective in enhancing blood circulation, which is particularly desired to keep inflamed parts less reddish. Apart from minimizing inflammation, this additionally decreases painful sensations and strains.

Massage therapy helps in draining excess fluid retention in affected body parts, ensuring that you feel comfortable after a minor or major injury while improving the mobility if a joint was affected. Although there are no substantiated claims on its benefits in increasing muscle strength, Massage Therapy does help in stimulating atrophied and weak muscles and joints, helping them get back to full shape.

By gently rubbing the skin, a massage expert promotes the release of endorphins, the popular "feel good" chemicals that also act as painkillers in the body. With less pain comes better sleep, and this promotes faster healing after an injury.

On the whole, massage has extensive effects on the autonomous nervous system which correlate to better stimulation and soothing of nerve endings. The resulting calming effect is felt by the whole body. As lymphs are invaluable parts of the circulatory system, ensuring that they are in good condition with increased activity for better toxin removal is what you want. The lymph also helps in replenishing lost supply of nourishment. The purification by lymph nodes purifies contents before they get to the heart.

Massage therapy has been shown to be incredibly effective in ensuring that all these processes occur seamlessly by enhancing the activity of the lymphatic system while preventing blockages and knots. Many individuals suffer from illnesses that are invariably caused or related to stress. Heart disease is one such problem that has continually plagued millions of people the world over in recent years. With the soothing effects of massage, individuals can improve their heart health as they feel more comfortable and better regulate their heart pressure.

POSITIVE APPLICATIONS

Massage therapy provides benefits in many applications, and arguably leading the pack here is in Complementary and Alternative Medicine (CAM) where it is used for:

1. Muscle spasms

2. Tension caused by headaches

3. Flaccid musculature

4. Reduced peripheral circulation

5. Lymphatic congestion

6. Anxiety

7. Backache

Apart from these proven benefits, some experts also believe that massage therapy can, directly or indirectly, be a phenomenal solution for other conditions such as:

1. Asthma

2. Allergies

3. Bronchitis

4. Osteoarthritis

5. Rheumatoid arthritis

6. Depression

7. Carpal Tunnel Syndrome

8. Gastrointestinal disorders

9. Insomnia

10. Myofascial pain

So, you may consider having a massage session to see the possible amazing results before embarking on a comprehensive treatment regimen. Having massage as part of your complementary alternative medicine can only be a great idea.

3
EDUCATION AND TRAINING

As with any professional skill, getting educated and enrolling in relevant training are fundamental to becoming a reliably qualified massage therapist. The caveat with massage therapy training, however, is that there is no laid down career paths to explore in becoming a massage expert. This is further compounded by the fact that training requirements and educational qualifications are not the same in all countries. Hence specifications differ from one country to another. In Canada, England and the United States, there are also noticeable differences in requirements among states and provinces. Some schools may additionally focus more on one type of massage therapy e.g. Sports, Swedish or Trigger-Point, but not the three. Hence, it is incumbent on the aspiring massage practitioner to find out what rules apply in the intended location of practice before enrolling in a massage course or training.

HOW TO CHOOSE A COURSE

While are there are key differences depending on the country of residence, a number of skillset and knowledge are vitally important in your armamentarium of massage therapy expertise. You should ensure to enroll in a program that covers all intricacies and nuances of the anatomy, physiology and kinesiology of the body as this will prepare a healthy ground for understanding the physical makeup of the body, its mechanics and motor development. Having a basic knowledge of biology can also be helpful if still in high school.

Apart from physiology related courses, your school of choice should get you acquainted with the many types of massage techniques we have today, including both Asian and American methods. A solid understanding of Swedish and Traditional

Chinese Massage is also key as you'll be more firmly positioned to take on any field in massage therapy since they cover most of the historical and dynamic massage techniques you need to know.

SPECIALIZING

Niching down to a particular speciality may sound alluring. And if that's what you want, there are more than a handful of schools offering programs specifically tailored to groom trainees on a particular type of massage therapy. With the basic knowledge acquired, you can easily zero in on a focal point as may be desired. Some specialities you may want to consider include Reflexology, Shiatsu, Reiki or Aromatherapy Massage. Trigger-Point, Sports or Swedish massage are other options to consider too. Hovering around your options for a decent period of time before going all in will ensure you don't delve deeper into a field that may ultimately be unappealing in the long run. However, if you don't feel the need to specialize, and becoming a general massage therapist sounds just fine, a general course should suffice.

WORKSHOPS

Workshops will likely help in narrowing down your options as they provide an insight into what you should expect in a specific niche. Most colleges and community centers offer many of these workshops, so leveraging this opportunity can be a hugely critical in helping evaluate your talent and personality to see if it strikes a chord before committing to a field of massage therapy.

PRACTICAL VS THEORY

Administering massage therapy sessions is more practical oriented than theoretical. So, enrolling in a school that provides the ample time for practicals is essential.

Theoretical classes will get you acquainted the history and basics of massage, but schools with more practical themed courses will likely ensure you have the requisite expertise to confidently take on massage therapy sessions after your program. So you want to ask the following questions before choosing a massage school.

- Does the school focus more on the practical or theoretical aspects of massage therapy?

- Are there a good deal of lessons and case scenarios to apply garnered knowledge?

- How about the provision of a learner-type program that helps you to solidify your theoretical knowledge in practical situations?

BUSINESS SKILLS

When you determine your course of post secondary education, look to see if the school offers courses in operating in the world of business. Such a curriculum will allow you to explore the options open to a massage therapist. These may include working in an office environment, alongside a chiropractor, out of your home or in your own office or shop. To help you make your decision, the ideal school will include financial courses. A reputable massage therapy school will provide you with information on such things as operating costs, location, financial options and how to prepare a business plan. A good massage school will also not ignore the topic of ethics both in business and with your clients. You need to be aware of these issues if you wish to be successful and the best possible massage therapist for your clients.

Massage schools may also help you obtain gainful employment. They can provide you with guidance in selecting employment. Some schools offer job placement services for their graduates. They also continue to support their alumni with specific services to help them continue their learning. This may include post-graduate courses or workshops.

ACCREDITATION AND LICENSING

Choose your school with care. Check to see if the courses you are taking are not only pertinent but are accredited. Since some states require licenses to operate, be sure you select a school meeting with their approval. Be aware, your education is ongoing. In some places, maintaining a valid license involves continually update your education and improving your skill through annual attendance at courses and workshops.

Be sure your school prepares you for the taking of any exams following your graduation. Some countries require you take a specific examination before you are able to operate in their jurisdiction. In the United States, you may be required to take the Certified Examination for Therapeutic Massage and Bodywork (NCETMB). In Europe and the United Kingdom, there are different licensing organizations and exams. The licensing requirements may actually vary in different cities. This may lead to confusion. The Irish Massage Therapists Association (IMTA), for example is trying to establish a national examination.

4
BASIC TYPES: EASTERN VERSUS WESTERN; TRADITIONAL VERSUS MODERN ECLECTIC

There are two basic types of Massage therapy: Western and Eastern. The Eastern form is also called Japanese, Chinese or Asian type. And while these two types of massage therapy share common similarities, a number of differences exist between both. However, the differences are not all a function of the origin but the philosophy behind the approach. For example, Western Massage traditionally involves sessions where the body is treated as a physical entity, following western ideals and reclining on western understanding medicine. However Asian or Eastern massage takes a more comprehensive approach by approaching sessions in a holistic way that considers the full entity of the body as one, thereby taking the emotional, physical and mental parts of the human being as different but singularly interdependent.

Both Eastern and Western Massage types have two subdivisions; traditional and modern eclectic forms. Traditional forms of massage are just as they sound, relying solely on the original concepts of massage, remaining strongly Western or Eastern in the treatment approach. On the other hand, modern eclectic massage therapy can be a blend of Western Massage techniques that utilize Eastern philosophy, or a juxtaposition between Eastern massage techniques and Western approach. Modern eclectic massage therapy is basically a variation in mix of both Massage types.

WESTERN MASSAGE THERAPY
Wester Massage was originally Swedish Massage or Classic Massage as it is called in Sweden. This type of massage therapy wholly centers on the medical or physical approach to treatment. Hence, western massage therapists are more concerned with the anatomy of body parts based on Western medical research.

The three main forms of Traditional Western Massage are:

- Medical Massage
- Sports Massage
- Deep Tissue Massage.

There are also a number of slight variations to these forms. These include:

- Hellerwork
- Esalen Massage
- Myofascial Release
- Trigger Point Massage or Myotherapy.
- Rolfing and

Thus the traditional western massage therapist primarily focuses on the physical maintenance or repair of the body as the case may be. For example, in Rolfing, a therapist focuses on the muscles and connective tissues to better realign the body. Esalen Massage, on the other hand, is a form of Swedish Massage that involves making rocking movements and gently stroking the deep tissues in a bid to restore the optimal functioning of body parts.

EASTERN MASSAGE THERAPY

Chinese or Asian Massage therapy is the sole discuss when Eastern Massage Therapy is mentioned. This massage type can come in a plethora of forms, with the most standard being acupressure. The approach employed here is entirely based off of Eastern medical and philosophical concepts where the healing of the body after an injury of any sort can only be possible by considering the whole life force referred to as Ki in Japanese and Chi or Qi in Chinese. The treatment involves ensuring a

delicate balance in all of a human's life force and thus deals with the mental, physical and emotional balance of man. This state of whole body balance is achieved by using a system that involves pathways or meridians.

In the Acupressure theory of Eastern Massage Therapy, it is believed that blocking any of the 8 channels or 12 meridians invariably leads to all forms of diseases and emotional imbalance. And to restore normalcy, an expert puts pressure on specific points of the body to enhance fluidity in the flow of energy, thereby restoring balance and improving overall health.

Some other traditional forms of Asian massage therapy are:

- Amma (Japan)

- Thai Massage

- Tuina or Tui Na (China).

These forms however do not deviate from the basic concept of Eastern methods of massage. For example, Tuina massage involves working with acupressure points to better stimulate the muscles and joints. Techniques involved include Chinese brushing, rolling, kneading and pressing.

MIXED

While both Western and Eastern forms of Massage therapy show slight variations, there are few combinations that exploit both methods; these are referred to as mixed or eclectic combinations. Some categories of mixed massage therapy include:

- Reiki

- Reflexology

- Aromatherapy Massage

- Shiatsu

Although forms like Reiki and Shiatsu have an approach that is heavily reliant on traditional oriental massage therapy or medicine, they all adopt more modern practices and are updated regularly. For example, Aromatherapy works by combining aromatic oils with different massage techniques.

Eastern or Western, all forms of massage therapy are tailored to promote good health, and only differ in their approaches. These distinct massage therapy types will be discussed in great depth in the next chapters, with a focus on their similarities, differences and everything in between. Some of these types of Massage Therapy we will be considering include the Swedish Massage, Deep Tissue Massage, Trigger- Point Massage, Sports Massage and Shiatsu.

Acupressure For Specific Problems

While acupressure does not hit a home run for all medical conditions, it does offer a worthy treatment technique that can be employed for successfully taking care of many conditions. Here are popular ways acupressure has been used to take care of specific health problems.

Colds and Flu

Colds are a common health challenge. Caused by viruses, colds and flu are not the best combination for a stress-free day. They are more likely to be experienced when favorable conditions of acidity, temperature, and moisture are available. When fatigued and low on immune defence capability, catching cold and flu are very likely, allowing the mucous membranes of the nostrils to provide a suitable ambience for the proliferation of viruses. Symptoms of cold occur as the body tries to prevent itself from attack by these invaders. This is essentially what causes a persistent runny nose when viruses enter the nostrils.

As acupuncture helps to speed up the process of expelling the virus, it may appear as though your symptoms are actually worsening. In reality, however, you are only going through the recovery process faster than occurs normally. While acupuncture will not expressly cure colds, it can hasten the recovery as well as confer decent protection against future attacks by working on specific points of the body.

The Bearing Support protein (Potent point B 36), located near the spine and off the tips of the shoulder blades, is particularly effective in helping the body develop better natural resistance to colds. Traditional Chinese medicine posit that cold and wind penetrate the skin at this protein points as the muscles tend to become tense before the onset of colds and flu.

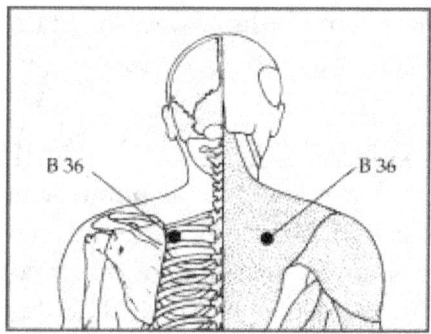

The following locations are the pressure points focused on when reversing cold and flu symptoms:

Drilling Bamboo (B 2)

Location: In the eye sockets' indentations, on either side of the point where the nose and the ridge of the eyebrows join.

Benefits: B2 helps to relieve sinus congestion and colds as well as fatigued eyes and headaches affecting the frontal region.

Facial Beauty (St 3)

Location: St 3 is located at bottom of the cheekbone and directly below the eye pupil

Benefits: Hastens recovery from congestion in the head, stuffy nose, fatigued and burning eyes as well as eye pressure.

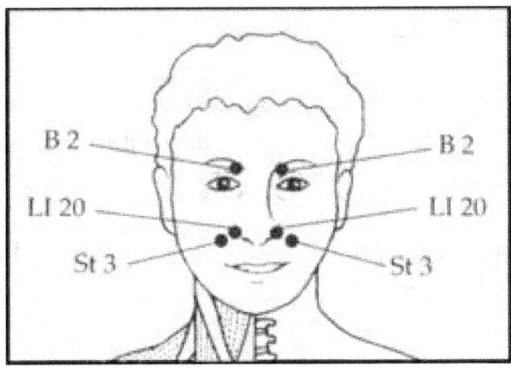

Welcoming Perfume (LI 20)

Location: On either side of the cheek, just outside the nostrils

Benefits: Reverses sinus pain, nasal congestion as well as facial swelling or facial paralysis.

Crooked Pond (LI 11)

Location: The Crooked Pond is found at the outer end of the elbow crease

Benefits: It helps to relieve the body of fever, symptoms of cold, elbow pain and constipation

Joining the Valley (Hoku) (LI 4)

Caution: The Hoku point is considered to be very sensitive, and so should not be touched by pregnant women as it could be stimulated to cause premature uteral contractions.

Location: It is located at the top end of the protruding muscle on the back of the hand when the index finger and thumb are in close proximity.

Benefits: Helps relief from flu, constipation, head congestion and headaches.

Gates of Consciousness (GB 20)

Location: GB 20 is located in the hollow of both sides of the base of the skull, two or three inches apart as dictated by the size of the head.

Benefits: Beneficial in relief from head congestion, headaches, neck pain, arthritis and irritability.

Wind Mansion (GV 16)

Location: This pressure point is located at the center of the back of the head, reclining in the spacious hollow under the base of the skull.

Benefits: Aids relief from red eyes, head congestion, headaches, mental stress and stiff neck.

Third Eye Point (GV 24.5)

Location: Between between both eyebrows, in the indentation where the nose bridge connects with the center of the forehead.

Benefits: Improves symptoms of head congestion, headaches and stuffy nose.

Elegant Mansion (K 27)

Location: Next to the breastbone, in the hollow just below the collarbone.

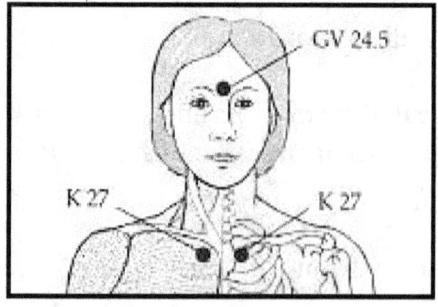

Benefits: Helps in breathing difficulties, chest congestion, coughing, and sore throats.

It is noteworthy, however, to only use one or two of the pressure points as time permits, but not all.

Step 1

Press into B 2: Using your thumbs, press on the upper eye ridge and into the slight hollow close to the nose bridge for one minute. Close your eyes and subsequently take some deep breaths while allowing the weight of the head to lean forward onto the thumbs.

Step 2

Press St 3 and LI 20: Place your middle fingers closely beside your nostrils and keep your index fingers close to them; Gently press up and underneath of your cheekbones for one minute. This step can easily be taught to kids to help in reversing nasal discomfort.

Step 3

Press both LI 11: Bend your right or left arm and place the thumb of the other hand at the end of the elbow crease on the outside of your forearm. Slightly curve your fingers and firmly press them into your elbow joint for a minute. Repeat these steps for the other arm.

Step 4

Press LI 4 firmly:

Spread apart your index and left thumb. Place your right thumb in the webbing like portion on the back of your left hand while leaving the fingertips on the palm directly behind your right thumb. Squeeze the webbing of your left hand by pressing your right thumb and index finger against the webbing, ensuring that the angle pressure is towards the bone connecting with the left index finger. Hold the position for one minute and switch hands.

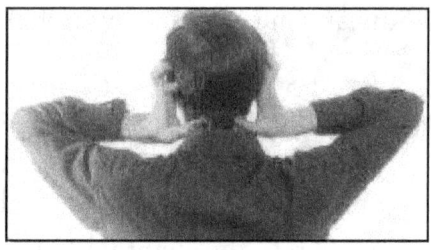

Step 5

Firmly press GB 20: Now close your eyes and place your thumbs underneath the base of your skull two to three inches apart. Slowly tilt your head back and apply pressure gradually, holding the position for one minute to fully release these important cold-relief points.

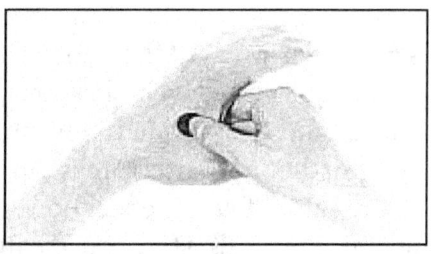

Step 6

Firmly press GV 16: Start by placing the tips of the middle fingers in the hollow at the center of the skull base. With your fingers kept on this point, inhale while tilting your head back and exhale as you lean forward. Continue the slow back and forth movement and

breathe deeply with this important point held in place for reversing symptoms of head congestion.

Step 7

Touch the GV 24.5: Bring the palms close together while ensuring that the middle and index fingers gently touch the Third Eye Point positioned between the eyebrows. Take a deep breath while holding this point to effectively balance your endocrine system

Step 8

Firmly press K 27: Gently place your fingertips on the collarbone protrusions and slide them down and outward into the first indentation in between the bones. Breathe deeply while pressing into this hollow and observe reversal of symptoms of congestion.

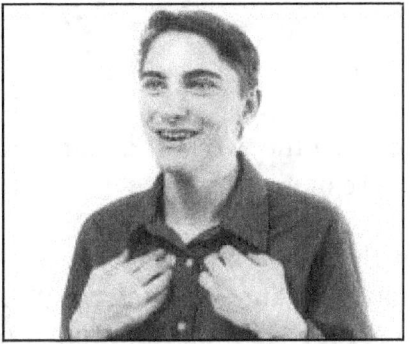

Headaches and Migraines

Headaches and Migraines can also be remediated by acupressure, and this process begins with locating some pressure points including:

Gates of Consciousness (GB 20)

Location: Underneath the base of the skull and two inches away from the middle of the neck.

Benefits: Reduces headache pains and pressure. Also helps reduce jaw and neck pain.

LV-3

Location:

On the top of the foot, in the valley region between the second and big toes.

LI-4

Location:

In the webbing separating the index finger and the thumb at the highest spot of the muscle when both index finger and thumb are brought in close contact.

TW-5

Location:

Between the two bones on the forearm, three finger widths above the crease of your wrist.

In the process of relieving yourself from migraine and headaches, start by taking a sitting position in a chair and bend over, ensuring that your elbows are propped on a desk or table. This position will enhance comfort when holding these points. Take deep breaths and firmly press the points for about 1 to 2 minutes.

Step 1:

Massage your head as though you are passing shampoo over your hair

Step 2:

Place the thumbs underneath the skull base on either position of the spinal column. Gently tilt your head backwards, breathe deeply and press upward for about two minutes.

Step 3:

Locate GB 20.

Ensure deep thumb pressure is applied for about a minute or more.

Step 4:

Locate LV 3.

Apply pressure on top of this spot using either your right heel or thumb and rub for at least one minute. Switch and repeat for the opposite foot.

For headaches affecting the forehead and regions above the eyes:

Locate Li 4.

Apply pressure on this spot for 2 minutes. Combine this with pressure on LV 3 for jaw relaxation.

For headache on temples or either side of the head:

Locate TW 5.

Apply pressure for two minutes. For general headaches

Carefully locate each of the above-outlined pressure points and apply deep pressure from the thumb to each for at least 2 minutes.

Chronic Back Pain

Chronic back pain can be reduced by identifying these pressure points:

B-123

Location: Slightly above the waist and about two finger widths on the two sides of the spine

B-140

Location: At the back in the middle of the crease.

B-157

Location: At the depression below the large muscle, just about halfway distance between the heel and crease of the knee.

B-160
B-161

Location: The dent on both sides behind the anklebone.

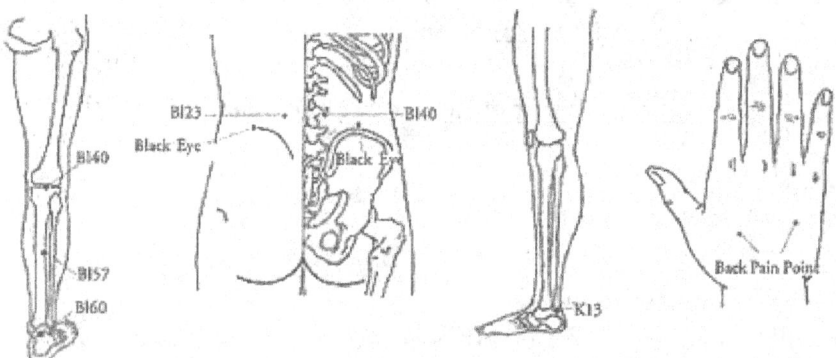

Step 1:

Stand erect with feet apart by a shoulder width. Place both hands on your back and use the palms of palm heels to gently stroke up and down from the wrist to the sacrum one hundred times.

Step 2:

Stand erect with feet shoulder

Stand with feet apart by a shoulder width. Put both hands on your back slightly below the waist. Ensure thumbs are positioned on two acupressure points called "Black Eyes." Press these points gently while slowly rotating the rest of your body left, right, forward and backward. Make loose fists and tap gently against these points for 1 minute.

Step 3:

Identify the spot where the most pain occurs and tap against this spot gently 30 times. Knead for 1 minute.

Step 4:

Press and knead B123 gently using your thumb and hold for about 1 minute.

Step 5:

Take a lying position on your stomach and ask someone else to gently press B140 with the thumb for 1 minute.

Step 6:

Knead and gently press B157 for 1 minute

Step 7:

Use both index finger and thumb to pinch B160Ki3. Repeat the process ten times.

Step 8:

Use thumb to gently press and knead the pressure point at the back of your hand, away from the crease of the wrist by two finger-widths.

One is between the middle and ring fingers and the other between the middle and index fingers ("Back Pain Point"). Practice this for 1 minute.

Weight Control

Acupuncture has been a reliable option for many conditions, and weight is another area where it can come incredibly handy too. The procedure can be performed shortly before you get up from bed in the morning or done after getting ready for sleep at night. For best results in controlling undesired weight, the following procedure should be performed once daily:

- Put the right palm on the bellybutton and the left on top of the right palm. In a counterclockwise direction, rub the abdomen outward 100 times.
- Place your left palm on the bottom and rub in a clockwise direction inwardly by starting from the outer edge of the abdomen. Repeat the process for the opposite side.
- Put your palms on the abdominal region and push down to the pubic region one hundred times.
- Put the right palm on the right rib's lower edge and push to the left groin area fifty times. Repeat the process for the opposite side.
- Finish your regimen by pressing and kneading your legs and arms for about ten minutes.

Here's another massage strategy for weight control:
- Pick up a long towel.
- Protect your skin by putting massage oil or cornstarch on your bare waist
- Stand firmly apart by a feet shoulder width and use the towel to wrap around the back of your waist.
- Firmly hold the towel ends and pull the towel back and forth so that it excellently scrapes across the waist.
- Continue this until heat is felt and skin flushing occurs.

The list of acupressure techniques has not been exhausted, with so many other variations and forms of acupressure helpful in relieving both minor and major discomforts. However, the aforementioned steps should get you started for most common conditions for which acupressure is quite effective.

5
COMMON TYPES OF MASSAGE THERAPY

Massage therapy can be performed in a number of ways, but according to the American Massage Therapy Association, five of these are the most commonly used today for the treatment of many conditions. These include Trigger Point, Swedish Massage, Deep Tissue, Shiatsu and Sports Massage. All of these but Shiatsu are western forms of Massage treatment, relying on key Western techniques to ensure the best massage results after a massage session.

SWEDISH MASSAGE

Classic Massage or Swedish Massage is one of the oldest western traditions that dates to as far back as the 10th century when Per Henrik Ling (1176 - 1839) made attempts to introduce the art of massage in sports education. For his goal, he combined many relevant Eastern healing techniques in his massage regimen that formed a unison with the western system of physiology, anatomy, and blood circulation. The current classical or traditional form of Swedish Massage was however further developed by Holland-born Johan Georg Mezger who also named the different kinds of strokes now known when applying Swedish Massage. These strokes include Petrissage, Effleurage, Tapotement and Friction.

- ☐ Petrissage involves kneading the flesh of an individual being massaged

- ☐ Effleurage refers to lightly touching and gliding smooth strokes

- ☐ Tapotement stoke or "tapping" has to do with alternating taps applied by applying cupped hands and fingers on the body

- Friction (rubbing) is the deep, circular movements to the soft tissue.

Vibration (shaking) can also be used by a massage therapist in addition to these four primary strokes.

Swedish Massage expectedly helps to improve relaxation, and consequently circulation. It is also helpful in better lubricating the joints and muscles, leading to increased flexibility due to enhanced range of motion. Massage experts and individuals alike find Swedish Massage a reliable way to ease stress while preventing mild to moderate injuries and stress-related diseases. Its improvement of circulation means this form of massage is also key in eliminating swollen regions due to injuries while additionally improving the ability of the lymphatic system to successfully carry out its functions. Hence healing turnaround is much faster as reduced welling facilitates better mobility of injured body parts. Although Swedish Massage stands as the traditional form of Western Massage, the growing demand for massage enthusiasts and experts have driven the creation of many variations of this Massage. The three popular variations of Swedish Massage commonly practised today are:

- Sports Massage

- Trigger Point Massage

- Deep Tissue Massage.

SPORTS MASSAGE

This popular variation of Swedish Massage has grown in popularity over the years. Due in part to the huge number of athletes demanding massage services more than ever before. Sports Massage includes some parts of Trigger Point Therapy and is applied to help athletes recover faster from injuries as well as prepare them to go to competitions with little to no injury fears. Designed for athletes,

Sports massage is done using a number of techniques including:

- ☐ Frictions

- ☐ Effleurage

- ☐ Petrissage

Compression and cross-fiber massage is another form that can be used for better muscle effects and increased flexibility. Sports Massage professionals may also employ Deep Tissue Friction (DTF) which became popular after its introduction by Dr James Cryiax. While it shows similarities with friction, DTF takes a deeper action and is applicable when tendon damage or injuries that lead to micro –tears and similar tendon and joint problems occur.

Although similar to Swedish Massage, Sports Massage is specifically designed to improve the abilities of athletes and its application is divided into 3 areas; Maintenance, Event and rehabilitation.

Maintenance Sports Massage helps athletes to train more competitively while significantly reducing the possibilities of coming down with injuries. On the other hand, Event massage is further split into three components: pre, inter and post. Pre Event massage involves all massage activities that are done to energize the blood and relaxe the muscles in preparation for a race or sporting event. Inter-Event massage is invaluable for checking any signs of damage to the body and also helps to get the body back in top condition for subsequent events. Post Event Massage is done for a much longer period of 1 to 2 hours and is designed to quicken recovery of tissues from stress and exhaustion after a competition.

However, the most commonly administered form of sports massage is rehabilitative massage which is geared at ensuring that athletes get their physical health back in full swing in the shortest time possible after sustained periods of sporting activities. It therefore works by stimulating key areas that help better circulation while reducing the time needed for complete restoration of balance to the whole musculoskeletal system.

As with many other forms of therapy, Sports Massage Therapy is beneficial for athletes of all ages. The end result is better performance, sustained balance and quick recovery after a stressful sporting activity.

TRIGGER POINT MASSAGE

Introduced by White House physician Janet Travell M.D. (1901-1997), Trigger Point massage is another popular form of Swedish Massage therapy. By releasing "Myofascial Pain and Dysfunction: The Trigger Point Manual" in 1983, Janet worked together with Simons to give a specific regimen, techniques, philosophy and purpose of the Trigger Point Massage. A fundamental belief of Trigger Point Massage is that pains are usually occasioned by small and tender congested knots residing in the muscles that act as trigger points.

These highly localized points were believed to cause insidious episodes of pains most of the time. These are pains like dull and throbbing aches that also include neck and jaw pain, headaches as well as joint and lower back pain. Trigger points have also been linked to symptomize carpal tunnel syndrome.

Other conditions associated with trigger points include dizziness, earaches, heartburn, nausea, sinus pain, colic in babies and congestion. The symptom definitive of a trigger point is what is referred to as "referred pain." Hence the trigger point may actually be symptomatic of a condition that may not have been triggered or started at the trigger point. In any case, the process of relieving trigger point stress and tension goes a long way in helping solve the problem by initiating the process of healing while breaking the pain-spasm-pain cycle. There are 3 fundamental regions recognized when Trigger Point Massage Therapy is given. These include satellite trigger points, central trigger points and attachment trigger points. There could also be a latent or active trigger point. And all of these have definitive effects that are pivotal in keeping the body healthy and pain free.

Applying pressure on the right trigger point therefore sets the ground for effective annulment of body pains wherever they may be emanating from. This is carried out in a way similar to what happens in Asian Acupressure where deep sustained pressure from the finger is applied to ease the balance and pains at the trigger points. Expectedly, the dynamic growth of Trigger Point Massage has ensured the development of slight variations and adaptations. There are two keep versions of Trigger Point Massage: Bonnie Prudden Myotherapy and Neuromuscular therapy.

DEEP TISSUE MASSAGE THERAPY

The third type of Swedish Massage is Deep Tissue Massage. This type is often regarded as more of a technique in contrast to being a specific form of therapy. Hence it finds relevance in many other types of massage therapy. While carrying out Deep Tissue Massage, an expert can take advantage of different kinds of techniques to successfully relieve the body of pains. The target of Deep Tissue Massage Therapy is specifically the myofascial connective tissue where adhesions can be found by the massage practitioner.

Adhesions are bands of tissue that are tight and rigid and are often a part of tendons, ligaments and muscles where they cause blockage of lymph and blood circulation.

The end result is pain that makes movement more difficult and triggers inflammation as the body tries to protect itself. In Deep Tissue Massage, the therapist tries to rid pains off the body by applying slow strokes accompanied by finger pressure on the adhesions or tight areas. The success of the approach is therefore dependent on applying sufficient pressure depth in these areas.

Deep Massage, like Sports Massage, has specific focus and intent as the therapist looks to realign the body's muscles and connective located at the deeper layers. A successful Deep Massage session can help relieve low back pains, carpal tunnel syndrome, inhibited movement in the joints and muscles, fibromyalgia and a host of chronic pains.

SHIATSU

In contrast to other aforementioned massage types, Shiatsu has an origin that can be traced to Eastern traditions. The word Shiatsu is Japanese and it is also referred to as a type of Chinese Acupressure. Shiatsu itself translates to "Finger pressure." Although inclined to some modern practices in Asian medicine, Shiatsu primarily has a traditional approach to human physiology and focuses on the entire being. Hence although invisible, the interconnection of the body, spirit, mind and emotion is considered in Shiatsu approach to massage therapy.

The Shiatsu technique demands a comprehensive knowledge of the interplay that exists between the Yin and Yang. Shiatsu Massage therapists are also required to be in the know of the existing interconnection between the body and Ki or the life force. The Ki is said to flow channels and meridians along which are Acupoints or Tsubo. A normal flowing Ki that is not impeded by obstructions or blockages means the body is exceptionally balanced and healthy. However, there are situations when Ki (Jitsu) can be excess or deficient (Kyo), in which case the body begins to feel pains with the onset of different illnesses and health problems.

One technique usually applied by a Shiatsu practitioner is tonification where a slow and gradual pressure is exerted on identified Kyo Meridians. The process helps to energize the meridians and consequently enhances the reversal of body pains. Jitsu can be relaxed in another variation where the therapist helps to treat pains using techniques as thumb pressure, palm pressure, elbow pressure and finger pressure. Yin refers to soft touch and sustained pressure while a rejuvenating and revitalizing touch is called Yang.

A good Shiatsu Massage session can, in addition to hasten reversal of symptoms, also help the hormonal body balance for better digestion and more effective reproductive systems. However, the specific goal is to ensure that Ki is delicately restored in balance to keep the body in good working condition. The versatile and awe effective nature of both Eastern and Western forms of Massage have predicated the consistent rise in demand for complementary and alternative medicine.

6
OTHER TYPES OF MASSAGE THERAPY: EASTERN

While there are popular types of Eastern Massage in common use, many options and alternative treatments abound for reversing pains and maintaining the integrity of the body. As informed earlier, the general divisions of massage types also have hybrids and modern variations that have been carved from existing forms of massage therapy. For example, both Eastern and Western Massage Therapy can be synergized for even more effective treatment.

Chinese Massage Therapy is the standard form of Eastern Massage Therapy and encompasses all aspects and practices linked to Chinese traditions. Energy Work or Asian Massage Therapy (AMT) are alternative terms used to describe CMT. AMT is a better description of this type of massage if you mean to include Thailand and Japan massage types. Common forms of pain relief using CMT include Amma, Tui Na or Acupressure.

The concept of AMT is hinged on the life force that travels along specific channels in the body (12 meridians and 8 other channels), and a disturbance of which is believed to cause physical, emotional and mental illness. When illness occurs, the massage practitioner restores normalcy by detecting the cause of the problem and explores appropriate techniques to restore Chi balance. These techniques include kneading, pressing, squeezing, percussing and pinching along the acupoints on the channels or extraordinary acupoints that are not on the channels. As this process is done to restore Ki/Qi balance which refers to the life or energy force, Eastern Massage Therapy is synonymously called Energy Work.

ACUPRESSURE

Acupressure is synonymous with Asian Massage Therapy; It is actually the most popular type of AMT. There are many variations of acupressure with both traditional and modern ones coming in different guises. For example, Amma (Japanese) and Tui Na (Chinese) are both traditional forms of acupressure, and although they both predate Shiatsu, they all share similar techniques. The principal technique employed in Amma acupressure is somewhat similar to Swedish Massage, with pressure point combination techniques combined with precise stroking of affected body parts. The healing is directed towards the meridians, and thus energy is channelled along these meridian points. Believed to likely have been based off of Tui Na practices, the theory of five elements is utilized in Amma acupressure.

Two thousand or more years old Tui Na precedes both Shiatsu ad Amma. The practice works with many different types of strokes. Some of these include waving, kneading, shaking, percussion, pressing and body manipulation at key pressure points in the body along specific meridians. Herbs may also be used when performing Tui Na acupressure.

Thai Massage bears some semblance with Tui Na but has its origin traced to both China and India. Although an Energy work, The pattern of meridian in Thai massage is peculiarly similar to the ancient form of Hindu energy work.

Palm pressure is exerted on specific points on the body along the meridians or channels to release any blockages and improve body balance. Thai Massage practitioners are also skilled in ensuring movement range is increased by energizing the body. Thai Yoga Massage is another blend that merges techniques in Thai Massage with Yoga poses. In Indian, the life force here is called Prana.

Modern forms of Asian Massage Therapy include Reiki and Aromatherapy massage. The origin of Aromatherapy massage can be traced to Egypt, India, Babylon, the Moorish Empire and Greece.

This type of massage is chiefly based on the power of scent from plant extracts of essential oils to drive the healing of body conditions. The techniques used may also differ, but are more of Swedish Massage than Tui Na.

Reiki, practitioners claim, has Tibetan origins. However, it has since gone on to become a reliable form of massage therapy with a variation today that was driven in the late 19th Century by Dr. Mikado Usui. Healing using the Usui system is based on the expert manipulation of energy. In contrast to "ki" which means the basic life

force, "Rei" is basically used to mean the universal aspect of healing. Reiki massage therapy is conducted via channels that are called Chakras and not meridians as in other forms of Asian Massage Therapy. And surprisingly, Reiki experts need not make body contact with the recipient of the therapy during the healing process.

7
OTHER TYPES OF MASSAGE THERAPY: WESTERN

So many forms of Eastern Massage Therapy have been discussed in the previous chapter, but Western Massage Therapy is not short of variations too. As said earlier, there are both modern and traditional forms of Western Massage Therapy. And while the popular ones include Trigger Point, Deep Tissue Massage, Sports Massage and Swedish massage, other options exist that can combine one or more forms of these Massage types to advance a more holistic approach to natural body healing. For example, you can have a mix of both traditional and western massage therapy, go for Swedish Massage variations, or simply carve a new form by combining elements from both Western and Eastern Massage Therapy. That said, other common forms of Western Massage Therapy include:

- Rolfing
- Esalen Massage
- Myofascial Release
- Medical Massage
- Kurashova Method
- Reflexology

The characteristic feature of Western Massage is that there is more focus on the body, with physical repair driving most techniques, especially in the case of Rolfing.

ROLFING

Ida P. Rolf (1896-1979) is the architect behind the art of Rolfing massage. A technique that is officially referred to as the Rolfing Method of Structural Integration which posits that shifts within the myofascial system or connective tissue are the lead causes of why wear down occurs in the body. Rolfing practitioners use the fingers, elbows and knuckles to help restore the body's natural alignment and therefore helps to prevent worsening of illnesses. A typical Rolfing therapy is completed after ten sessions. A hitherto painful procedure, Rolfing has since been modified to ensure all clients have the best and equally convenient healing process.

Having practised at the Esalen Institute in California, Ida Rolf proceeded to establish her own school and method called the Rolf Institute. As is Rolfing, Esalen massage is rooted on techniques similar to Swedish Massage. Hence, it also features long strokes, but in combination with deep tissue massage aided by gentle rocking movements in what is called a nurturing or caring environment.

Myofascial Release Massage Therapy isn't dissimilar to Rolfing and is credited to the efforts of Physical therapist John Barnes. The focus is also on the fascia, hence the therapist restores balance to the body by releasing tension using the palms, fingers, elbows and forearms. Techniques involving long, gliding and smooth strokes are employed in the process. Myofascial Release Massage Therapy may also be incorporated into other Massage Therapy types.

MEDICAL MASSAGE

Another variation of Swedish Massage is Medical Massage which is typically concerned with healing the physical body. However, it can be approached in various ways and techniques as dictated by the patient's condition and physician's directions or prescriptions. Hence Medical Massage experts work in synergy with other health experts to achieve the goal of healing from a wide range of conditions including tennis elbow, deformities, knee pain, sciatica, repetitive stress disorders and sprained ankles.

Medical Massage based on the Kurashova Method can be traced to Russia from where it was introduced to the United States by Zhenya Kurashova Wine. There are over one hundred strokes in the Kurashova Method and the type of stroke applied, whether deep of gentle, is a function of the condition suffered by patients. The Kurashova method synergises elements of both Sports and Medical Massage Therapy.

REFLEXOLOGY

Although regarded as a form of Eastern Massage Therapy with origins linked to Chinese Acupuncture and Egyptian wall paintings, Reflexology was actually founded by Americans. Dr. William Fitzgerald came up with a theory that sought to define a way to keep the body in proper condition. His proposal was based on the interconnection of unique points on the feet, pressure and effect on organs in the body. Fitzgerald referred to 10 specific zones that, if pressed correctly, would greatly help in maintaining the integrity of body organs and keep people healthy. A similar theory to the concepts of Chinese Massage where these points are otherwise called meridians and channels.

To further this theory, American Masseuse Mrs Eunice D. Ingham spearheaded the adoption of Fitzgerald's ideas. This culminated in her 1998 published book *The Stories the Feet Can Tell* after which the art of Reflexology Massage became popular.

Reflexology believes specific foot points have links to organs in the body, and that by pressing these points, healing of pains and similar conditions is possible. Reflexology is naturally combined with aspects of both Eastern and Western Massage forms of Therapy like Shiatsu, Aromatherapy, Chinese Massage Therapy, Sports Massage and Yoga.

8
TERMINOLOGY

Here are common terms used in Massage Therapy and their meanings.

Acupressure:

A Chinese Traditional Massage method that involves using the fingers to apply pressure on key points along the meridians or Qi or Ki energy channels. Shiatsu is one such example of Chinese Traditional Massage Therapy that employs Acupressure.

Amma:

Amma or Anma is Japan's traditional massage therapy. It precedes Shiatsu and is based on Traditional forms of Chinese massage, employing techniques like stroking, acupressure, percussion and kneading along the meridians.

Aromatherapy Massage:

A type of Massage that uses scents from essential oils to reinvigorate the senses and promote healing.

Asian Massage Therapy:

A broad term that refers to forms of Massage Therapy with forms of Eastern or Oriental origins. In contrast to Western Massage Therapy, Asian Massage does not focus exclusively on the physical body but applies a more holistic approach that considers the interrelatedness of the soul, mind, emotion and body in the healing process. This form of therapy is also reliant on Asian or Oriental traditional concepts of physical and medical properties on the anatomy of the body. The process beliefs in the need to balance the life force or energy level referred to as Qi, Ki or Chi. And by examining the energy flow along the Chakras, Meridians or Channels, the expert can correctly determine where to stimulate by using techniques as kneading to balance the energy flow. Asian forms of Massage Therapy include Tui Na, Shiatsu, Amma and Thai Massage.

Ayurveda:

Refers to a system of healing based on ancient Indian Vedic writings. A classic example of healing by Ayurveda method is Deepak Chopra. The system also employs massage therapy for a comprehensive healing approach.

Chakras:

An often used terminology by Reiki practitioners. Chakras is a concept used to refer to one of the seven centers regulating energy flow between the body and mind.

Channels:

Channels, sometimes called meridians, are the invisible pathway of energy flow within the body. The term is commonly used in Asian or Eastern Massage Therapy.

Chi:

Chi is a Chinese word that refers to life force or energy and is thus central in the restoration process of overall health involving the body, emotions and mind in Chinese Medicine. An overabundance of Chi, blockage, or paucity of it is negatively impactful on the health. Hence, Chi practitioners work to balance the Chi in cases where an individual is ill. Qi is another Chinese word for Chi. In Japanese, Ki is used instead. In Indian Massage practices, Prana is the word used to mean Chi.

Connective Tissue Massage:

Developed in Germany in 1930, Connective Tissue Massage works on the tissue layers between the skin and muscle to restore effective functioning and flexibility to the muscle layers. The therapy holds that there is a positive ripple effect on other parts of the body having effectively massaged one part.

Deep Tissue Massage:

A massage type that focuses on manipulating the myofascial connective tissue. Deep Tissue Massage, apart from being a form of Massage, is also a technique employed in other types of massage therapy. The massage is reliant on Structural Integration and Swedish Massage Therapy.

Eastern Massage Therapy:

Check Asian Massage Therapy.

Effleurage:

A Swedish Massage technique that involves using both hands in driving smooth and gliding strokes on parts of the body for a calmer and soothing experience.

Esalen Massage:

Developed at the Esalen Institute in California, Esalen Massage combines Swedish Massage elements with principles involving sensory awareness and environmental sensitivity.

Fascia:

Refers to the connective tissues providing the support needed by the muscles, bones, and body organs.

Friction:

A principal Swedish Massage Therapy technique, friction involves deeper skin penetrations by using the hand to make circular motions during a massage session.

Hot Stone Massage:

A massage technique where heated stones of different sizes are placed on the body to aid healing. Massage experts often do this in combination with Asian Massage Therapy like Shiatsu, in which case the stones are positioned on targeted channels, meridians, chakras and pressure points.

Ki:

The Japanese word for Chi i.e. the energy or life force of the body.

Kurashova Method:

A method employed in Russian Medical Message that includes more than 100 types of strokes applied on affected body parts to ease pain and quickens recovery in Athletes.

Medical Massage:

A type of Swedish Massage where physicians prescribe or direct needed medical forms of therapeutic massage depending on the injury presented by an individual.

Meridians:

Also called Channels or Chakras, they refer to the pathways directing the flow of energy or life force in the body. They are the center of focus in most forms of Asian Massage Therapy.

Myofascial Release:

A massage technique wherein the fascia is worked on using the elbows, fingers, hands, palms and forearms to make smooth, slow and long strokes to increase mobility of the fascia.

Oriental Massage Therapy:

Check Asian Massage Therapy

Petrissage:

A Swedish Massage technique that involves kneading the flesh.

Prana:

The Indian word for Chi which stands for life force or energy.

Reflexology:

A massage that concentrates on hands and feet. In reflexology, the expert forces pressure on specific zones of the limbs in a bid to release tension, stress, or pain in these body parts.

Reiki:

Based on Asian methods of massage and medicine, Reiki is characteristically different as it doesn't require the practitioner to use the hands during the healing process. Experts only transfer energy from the hand to the affected parts when restoring balance by using the concepts of Chakras and life forces.

Rolfing:

By deeply manipulating the body's myofascial system, the rolfing technique is a structural integration method that helps to reorganize the structure of the body after a muscle injury or strain.

Rosen Method:

The Rosen Method employs noninvasive touch and verbal communication to help patients recover from an illness. Massage or touch is used to detect any aberrant muscular contraction predicating a health problem while verbal communication is used to find out underlying emotional problems.

Shiatsu:

Meaning "finger pressure" in Japanese, it is a form of Acupressure that involves restoring energy balance to the Ki meridians or channels by applying pressure. It is a popular method of healing in Asian and Western cultures.

Sports Massage:

Another Swedish Massage variant that differs in the area of massage application. In contrast to the entire body as occurs in Swedish Massage, Sports Massage focuses on specific regions of the body and helps to restore and improve as well as rehabilitate and maintain the health of athletes. The three subdivisions of Sports Massage are Maintenance, Event and Rehabilitation. There are also variations. For example, Equine Sports Massage which is specifically designed for racing horses.

Structural Integration:

A term that is primarily used to describe Rolfing. However, Structural Integration can be used to mean other massage therapy and bodywork that involves integration of the body structure. Deep Tissue Massage, for example, employs the technique of Structural Integration.

Swedish Massage Therapy:

The key type of Western Massage Therapy that focuses on

physically healing the body. Swedish Message Therapy is the source of other popular massage types like Sports Massage, Deep Tissue Massage, Rolfing and Medical Massage. Techniques used in Swedish Massage Therapy include Petrissage, Effleurage, Tapotement and Friction.

Tapotement:

Tapotement is a Swedish Massage Technique that involves healing by using the edge of the hand, fingers, or cupped hands to make gentle strokes on affected body parts in quick, alternating taps.

Thai Massage:

A popular type of Asian Massage Therapy that uses principles of Eastern or Oriental Medicine. The massage is done by carefully manipulating the body using a number of other techniques like acupressure. Thai Massage can also be done in combination with Yoga in what is called Thai Yoga Massage.

Trigger Point Massage Therapy:

A massage therapy that uses the "Trigger Points" concept where certain points are believed to the centers of certain muscles that are essential in radiating pains to the whole body. Hence the message therapy is focused on expertly pressing these points to relieve body pains. A variation of this Massage Therapy is Bonnie Prudden Myotherapy.

Tui Na:

A form of Chinese Massage Therapy that uses Traditional healing concepts, Tui na helps to reverse health problems by employing the Chi or Qi life force that flows along channels or meridians in the body using techniques as rubbing, acupressure, pressing, waving, percussion, shaking and manipulation.

Western Massage Therapy:

A Massage term based on Western concepts and understanding of the anatomy and physiology of the body. Traditional Western Massage Therapy solely focuses on the physical body and thus differs from Eastern or Asian Massage therapy that takes a more holistic approach to body healing. Western Massage Therapy comes in many forms including Sports Massage, Swedish Massage and Medical Massage.

Zones:

A reflexology term that defines manipulation points explored by a massage practitioner to douse stress, reinvigorate the body after an exercise and restore the general health of individuals. Each foot or hand zone is connected to a central part or organ of the body.

CONCLUSION

The art of Massage has made tremendous progress over the years, with robust services that are no longer exclusively provided in unsavory parlous and locations. It has also evolved to be a healthy session for everyone, and not a service that is specially made for some elite group of individuals as was the case in the past. Its far-reaching benefits have ensured that basic coverage of many health plans now include massage therapy.

A myriad of issues can successfully be treated by going for a massage session, and this includes many injuries and emotional health concerns. In Sports Massage, for example, athletes can better recover from strains and muscle problems that are synonymous with sporting activities. This positions athletes to hit a home run in subsequent events. Chronic pains of varying sorts can also be rescinded with a carefully done massage therapy. Mothers who have just been delivered of babies can benefit from the calming benefits needed to take on postpartum depression.

Becoming a massage professional comes with a few challenges, and popular concerns have been based on licensing requirements and courses needed to fully practice the art of massage. This is partly due to the overwhelming options available and niche areas that can be specialized on. For example, Asian Massage Therapy focuses on a holistic healing principle that can be carried out in many ways. Western Massage, on the other hand, is concerned with the total physical entity, with forms like Swedish, Medical and Sports all yours in the taking. There is also Reflexology and Reiki that are eclectic in nature, combining aspects of Asian and Western traditions.

The healing properties of massage seem to be constantly expanding, and with more research unravelling hitherto unknown benefits, the massage rave will likely not wane in the nearest future.

With that, we have come to the end of this book. I want to thank you for choosing this book.

Now that you have come to the end of this book, we would first like to express our gratitude for choosing this particular source and taking the time to read through it.

All the information here was well researched and put together in a way to help you understand the massage therapy principles as easily as possible.

We hope you found it useful and you can now use it as a guide anytime you want. You may also want to recommend it to any family or friends that you think might find it useful as well.

www.ingramcontent.com/pod-product-compliance
Lightning Source LLC
Chambersburg PA
CBHW052158110526
44591CB00012B/1997